A CONTEMPORARY
MEDITATION
ON HOPE

A CONTEMPORARY MEDITATION ON HOPE

by JOHN HEAGLE

THE THOMAS MORE PRESS

ACKNOWLEDGMENTS

The author wishes to thank the following for permission to quote material from their publications.

Excerpts from *The Jerusalem Bible*, copyright © 1966 by Darton, Longman & Todd, Ltd. and Doubleday and Company, Inc. Used by permission of the publisher.

Lines from *Stolen Apples* by Yevgeny Yevtushenko. Translation copyright © 1971 by Doubleday & Company, Inc. Used by permission of Doubleday & Company, Inc.

Lines from *The People, Yes* by Carl Sandburg © 1936 by Carl Sandburg. Used by permission of Harcourt, Brace, Jovanovich, Inc.

Excerpt from *Orthodoxy* by G. K. Chesterton. © 1936 by G. K. Chesterton. Image Book edition, 1959. Used by permission of Doubleday & Company, Inc.

Lines from *Love and Fame* by John Berryman, © 1970 by Farrar, Straus & Giroux, Inc. Used by permission of the publisher.

Excerpt from *What God Has Joined Together* by Gustave Thibon. © 1952 by Gustave Thibon. Used by permission of Henry Regnery Co.

Excerpts from *The Phenomenon of Man* by Teilhard de Chardin. © 1961 by Harper & Row. Used by permission of Harper & Row, Inc.

Excerpt from *Neither Victims Nor Executioners* by Albert Camus. © 1972 by Dwight MacDonald published by World Without War Publications. Used by permission of Dwight MacDonald.

Lines from "The Lesson for Today" from *The Poetry of Robert Frost* edited by Edward Connery Lathem. Copyright © 1942 by Robert Frost. Copyright © 1969 by Holt, Rinehart and Winston, Inc. Copyright © 1970 by Lesley Frost Ballantine. Reprinted by permission of Holt, Rinehart & Winston, Inc.

For my mother and father

CONTENTS

Chapter One

UNLESS A GRAIN OF WHEAT FALLS
INTO THE GROUND AND DIES

Hope: The Language of the Earth

In an age which offers a variety of escapes from the human condition the Christian is more than ever a sign of contradiction. He continues to believe that the search for God must begin with the acceptance of the human. He believes this because it is in the stable of humanity that God has come in search of man.

In the human experience of Jesus, God became available to us as the depth of human life. Thus, a Christian believes that the experience of ultimate meaning comes not from a leap out of the human condition, but in a journey through its dark waters. This is simply another way of saying that a Christian shares the passover journey of Christ. A Christian believes that his life at this time, in this place, whatever the circumstances, is going somewhere. No matter the ambiguity and the darkness, the suffering and the uncertainty, he trusts that his journey is ultimately an experience of *good* news. A Christian stakes his life on this conviction. He does so in the face of many other beliefs and attitudes toward human life: some which experience it as absurd and empty, others that seek to wall it off from any transcendent ground, and still others which seek only for a means to escape from it. The Christian, on the other hand, literally bets his life on the transforming power of the incarnation. He commits himself to the task of giving human shape to his search for meaning. Together with God he chooses to let his word take flesh. Together with Jesus he "casts out into the deep" of the human ocean (cf. Lk 5:4).

There is a name for this inward stance of the Christian. We call it hope. Hope is another word for casting out into the deep. Hope is the way a Christian's word takes flesh. Hope is the willingness of man to follow God into the world. A Christian, says St. Paul, is one who lives by hope.

I am a man who claims for himself the name Christian. I claim it not as a title I deserve, but as a gift I am trying to receive, as a summons I choose to follow. I claim the name Christian, not as a social label or as a religious category, but as a process of soul and a commitment of life. I am a person in search of the good news at the center of my life. In fellowship with my brothers and sisters, I am struggling to discover the loving presence at the center of my existence and to share the passover journey of the Son as he continues to move through the undercurrent of human life toward resurrection. I am choosing to stake my life on his journey. I am a person who is learning how to hope.

To learn how to hope is to find ourselves moving

between two polarities of experience: human life and the gospel. On the one hand, we must try to read the gospel in the light of our human experience; on the other hand, we must try to understand our lives in the light of the gospel. As human beings we test the gospel in the crucible of life; as Christians we are tested daily by the humanness of the gospel.

Everything I know about hope arises from this encounter between gospel and life. I have experienced hope in the unfolding of my life and in the relationships I share with others. I have experienced hope in the struggle and growth of the earth upon which I walk. But it is only the gospel which gives direction and significance to all these experiences. When the gospel finds a place at the center of our lives it enfleshes itself as a stance of hope. When the gospel touches the heart of man, hope becomes the leaven of experience and the language of life.

Hope is the language of the earth.

The earth that I've walked and shared with others for most of my life is a great river valley. The native Americans long ago named it Mississippi—"Father of Waters." In this valley there are reflected the movements and struggles of all the earth. Like the shores and hills, the plains and mountains of other people's lives, this valley is a microcosm of the earth's mystery and power.

In our part of the valley the seasons unfold in well-defined rhythms. They pulse like deep-running moods through the land. From one perspective they appear as distinct and contrasting forces of life and death. Summer is a teeming burst of sunlight and greenery; winter, a snow-covered expanse of silence. One can only appreciate the clear stillness of a January night if he can remember the warm evenings of August, when the air moves as slowly as the river.

But if there is contrast, there is also convergence. If July and January stand in relief as life and death, heat and cold, light and darkness, then April and October are seasons of struggle when nature encounters the power of the earth in transition. Summer and winter are experienced as contrasts only because autumn and spring are experienced as collisions—great, struggling encounters of the elements and forces of the earth.

There comes a day in late August or early September when there is a hint of crispness in the air. Soon the geese are flying southward buffeted by the October wind. There is the glorious eruption of autumn color; then, almost as suddenly, the stillness of snow.

There comes a day in late February or early March when the sky takes on a softness. There is something about the air and the look of the sun. Soon the creeks and tributaries swell with melting snow. Spring comes as a burst of new life. Then it is summer.

The seasons of transition speak their own word about hope and life. In the autumn it is a story about the tenacity of life. People sometimes think of autumn as a gentle time when death comes easily. Gentleness is a part of autumn. There are the leaves that fall and do so quietly: the maples, the poplars, the ash, the beeches. But there is also the oak. Unlike other trees that lose their leaves, many of the oak leaves cling with tenacity through the brisk winds of October and even through the winter storms. Oak leaves do not die easily. In the image of Dylan Thomas they "do not go gentle into that good night." It is only the surge of new life in spring, the first warmth of new growth, that forces them to let go. They fall to their death only on the edge of a promise. The autumn oak speaks of a hope that will not surrender except to new life.

The season of spring expresses yet another word about hope. It speaks of the power and the presence of death as it collides with the forces of new life. I know that poems and songs have been written about the quiet ease with which new life appears. But in this valley spring often comes as an upheaval rather than a smooth transition. I recall walking near the banks of the river in early March after the first hint of spring. I could hear the deep-throated groans of the ice beginning to crack and to heave. Spring does not come with a gentle shrug but with a wrenching and a surging. When the river finally breaks free, sometimes in destructive floods, it flows as though in victory after a great struggle.

Hope is the language of the earth. The earth speaks of hope by what it says about life. It says that life is full of rhythms and cycles, of contrasts and moods. Like the river valley, life sometimes whispers its movement, while at other times it erupts in a burst of power and vitality. The earth speaks of growth and transition, the struggle and striving in the valleys and hillsides of men's lives. It also speaks of an underlying purpose and direction. Beneath the changing moods of the seasons there is the steady flow of the river. The river speaks of a constancy at the depth of life. It is the same river that mirrors the green foliage of summer and that moves hidden and silent beneath the winter ice. The earth speaks of hope by enfleshing the mystery of growth, and by expressing that growth in the form of struggle. It speaks of hope because it reveals that dying is not separate from living, and that living is at the heart of all dying. Hope is the language of the earth because it reveals what Hopkins expressed in poetic insight: "There lives the dearest freshness deep down things."

Hope is the poetry of the human condition.

Pascal once wrote that "rivers are roads that move and take us wherever we wish to go." Those who live along the rivers and hillsides and fields of the earth see reflected in the contrasts and struggles, the movements and upheavals of the earth—their own lives. In the seasons they experience the moods and currents of their deeper selves. They scan the horizon for signs of hope. They search for the direction of the river that flows through the human condition.

I have learned about hope not only from the earth I walk on, but also from the people whose lives speak the poetry of the human search. They are people who are willing to leave the surface of life and move towards its frightening center. I think of them now because they open their lives to the forces and movement of the earth. They let the gospel permeate them so that the Word might enflesh itself in their lives. Like the earth upon which they walk, their lives have the seasons of contrast—the struggle between life and death, light and darkness, sadness and joy. They also have the seasons of transition—the upheavals and the tensions, the tenacious clinging to life, and the final letting go. I think of them now because they embody the meaning of Christian hope: students who grope toward their identity with determination and endurance; husbands and wives who learn through years of self-giving that marriage is a covenant sealed in pain and growth; religious and priests who experience the upheaval of change in the Church and yet keep on walking into the future. St. Paul was speaking for these pilgrims of hope when he wrote: "We can even boast about our sufferings. These sufferings bring patience, as we know, and patience brings perseverance, and perseverance brings hope and this hope is not deceptive because the love of God has been poured into our hearts by the Holy Spirit which has been given us" (Rm 5:3–5).

Hope is the Word made flesh.

If hope is the language of the earth and the poetry of human experience, it is only because God's Word has drawn near to men. "The Word was made flesh, and lived among us." This simple statement in the prologue of John's gospel is the basis for approaching the human as the sacrament of the divine. In Jesus, God pitched his tent with men. Throughout the course of his life Jesus experienced the pain and the beauty, the agony and the promise of being human. He discovered that the depth of human life is not an experience of absurdity or a midnight void, but an encounter with a personal presence. Jesus addressed this loving presence as "Abba"—Father. He invites those who follow him to share this same relationship, to embrace life as a loving communion. He summons them to become sons and daughters of the same Father and he hands over his Spirit to make that possible.

The meaning of the earth's struggles and seasons, the poignancy of the human search are hollow, even empty without the mystery of the incarnation. It is because the Word has become flesh that we must take the earth and the human condition so seriously. It is because of the incarnation that Teilhard de Chardin could pray: "Lord Jesus, come to us clothed in the glory of the world."

The gospels are accounts of Jesus, the human God. They describe his struggle to follow the call of his Father and to communicate the depth of his experience to those who believe in him. The style and form of Jesus' words tell us how seriously he took the human journey. When Jesus speaks of man encountering God he uses earthy and human langauge. He does not speak of trusting the Father or loving one's brother in the abstract. On the contrary, he urges his followers to experience the presence of the Father in the world around them and in their relationships with one another. The gospels are filled with the language of the earth and of human experience. Jesus' words are the language of a rabbi who never forgot that he was a carpenter's son. His

words are full of the sounds and colors and contrasts
of the earth: salt and candles, yeast and coins, weeds
and wheat, wood and sand, nets cast into the sea,
pearls hidden in the earth, birds and sunsets, trees
and storms, bread and wine. The gospels, like the
river valley, speak the language of the earth.

The gospels also describe the struggling and
searching of human beings. Jesus reaches out to the
blind, the lame, the tax collectors, the prostitutes,
the fishermen, the soldiers and the pharisees. They
do all the human things like working and laughing,
weeping and sweating, dying and thirsting, worry-
ing and being afraid, and yes, hoping.

It is not surprising that Jesus chose to describe
the final meaning of his life in earthy images. As his
hour drew near he spoke of his passage to the Father
in the language of the earth: "Now the hour has
come for the Son of man to be glorified. I tell you
most solemnly, unless a wheat grain falls on the
ground and dies, it remains only a single grain: but
if it dies, it yields a rich harvest. Anyone who loves
his life loses it. Anyone who hates his life in this
world will keep it for the eternal life. If a man
serves me, he must follow me. Wherever I am, my
servant will be there, too" (Jn 12:23–26).

Jesus sees the grain of wheat as a metaphor of
human experience. He is not just giving his disciples
a moral injunction regarding self-sacrifice. He is
doing much more. He is describing his life's journey
as the new and final exodus. Jesus *is* the grain of
wheat. He chooses to fall into the ground and die
that he might bring forth new life. By falling into

the ground and dying a grain of wheat is transformed into a new sheaf. In the same way, the resurrection of Christ is the birth of a new humanity.
Christ becomes the Church. Out of the soil of the
earth, out of the heart of the human condition, hope
has arisen.

Jesus is the eternal Word of God spoken in human
flesh. Because he is the Word of *God,* he reveals the
presence and inner life of the Father. Because he is
the Word made *flesh,* he is also the revelation of
man. Jesus not only taught us how to call God our
Father but also how to recognize men as our brothers and the earth as the true soil beneath our feet.
God's embrace of the human condition is the beginning of hope within that condition.

There is a tendency to believe that the test of
Christian faith is our willingness to accept Jesus as
the Son of God. Belief in Christ's divinity is a central
doctrine of Christianity. But the Christian is also
called to believe that Jesus is man. The earliest, and
one of the most persistent heresies in the Church is
not the denial of Christ's divinity, but the refusal to
believe in his humanity. Because we find it difficult
to accept our own humanity, we are uneasy with a
God who takes on our human condition. John the
Baptist's words are true of every generation: "In
your midst, there is someone whom you do not
know." That someone who comes to us in the flesh,
that someone whom we do not recognize, is not only
the Lord, it is ourselves.

Some of the early Christians were tempted to
locate the reason for their hope outside the human

condition. They could accept Jesus as the Son of God, but they could not bring themselves to believe that he was truly man. This early denial of Christ's humanity is called Docetism—the belief that Jesus only "seemed" to be human. In response to this attitude John wrote to his fellow Christians: "Something which has existed since the beginning that we have heard and we have seen with our own eyes; that we have watched and touched with our hands: the Word who is life—this is our subject. That life was made visible: we saw it and we are giving our testimony, telling you of the eternal life which was with the Father and has been made visible to us. What we have seen and heard, we are telling you so that you, too, may be in union with us as we are in union with the Father and with his son, Jesus Christ. We are writing this to you to make our own joy complete" (I Jn 1–4).

John could only speak of Jesus from his experience. Jesus was a person John had seen and heard and touched. This is the only way any Christian can speak of Jesus—from the human experiences that touch him and shape him and become visible in his life. We are in union with Jesus and the Father only when we are united with other men in the ever-present struggle between joy and pain in our lives.

Any reflection on Christian hope must begin with the mystery and language of the incarnation. There are many forms and varieties of hope that men pursue. There are blind hopes and vague hopes, delayed hopes and frustrated hopes. There are many people who hope that the world might go away, or that they might get away from the world. That is not the hope that we are reflecting on here. The Christian is not one who is trying to stop the world in order to get off; he is striving to follow the journey of Christ into the heart of the human experience. Christian hope is born in the human condition and grows up in it in order to walk through it. Anything else may be blind optimism or wishful thinking but it is not Christian hope. To speak of Christian hope, we must leave the world of abstraction and enter the world of breathing and hurting and laughing and crying human beings. We must embrace the earth upon which they walk.

Only a few years ago, we were praising the virtues of the secular city with its skyscrapers and its technology as a means of the coming of God's kingdom. In the meantime our technology has begun to threaten our humanity. Today we are painfully aware that we must listen again to the language of the earth in order to discern the direction of the future. It is true that we are called to come of age and to take responsibility for history. But we cannot afford to forget that we are earthlings before we are cosmopolitans. A few years ago, it would have been considered romantic or even sentimental to speak of hope as the language of the earth. Now, we find ourselves looking to the earth with sober realism, for as our links with the earth become more distant, they also become more tenuous. Suddenly, we are listening again to the movement and process of the earth. We are trying to hear what it says about the limits and possibilities of being human, about our hopes and about our history. Our science enabled us to go to the moon. Our vision from that satellite enabled us to rediscover the earth. We saw again the fragility and gentleness of the earth, its miracle of life. We rediscovered our human condition with its beauty, as well as its burden.

Several years ago a close friend gave me a gift which I have continued to treasure. It is a piece of driftwood, shaped by nature's forces into the form of a cross. My friend found this driftwood cross on the banks of the Mississippi. It has become an important symbol of hope for me. It speaks the language of the earth. It expresses the poetry of the human condition. It tells me of the Word made flesh. It is a symbol of the strong, steady growth of wood as it unfolds through the seasons. At its center is a contradiction and a collision where one branch has grown together with another. The gnarled and twisted center speaks of the struggle that is at the heart of the cross. It expresses the tenacity with which life clings to life.

"The earth," says Robert Frost, "is the right place for love." The earth is not only the right place for love, it is also the right place for hope. It is, in fact, the only place where hope can begin. It is the only place where hope can be nourished and grow and break through to the gift of eternal life.

Chapter Two

A TIME TO BE BORN
The Season of Hope

For everything its season, and for every activity under heaven its time:

> a time to be born and a time to die;
> a time to plant and a time to uproot;
> a time to kill and a time to heal;
> a time to pull down and a time to build up;
> a time to weep and a time to laugh;
> a time for mourning and a time for dancing;
> a time to scatter stones and a time to gather
> them;
> a time to embrace and a time to refrain from
> embracing;
> a time to seek and a time to lose;
> a time to keep and a time to throw away;
> a time to tear and a time to mend;
> a time for silence and a time for speech;
> a time to love and a time to hate;
> a time for war and a time for peace.

Ecclesiastes 3:1–8, *New English Bible*

This poem is one of the most popular and well-known passages in the Old Testament. The author, whose name and background are unknown, is a mysterious figure who lived and wrote about three centuries before Christ. He introduces himself only as Qoheleth—"The Preacher," which is simply the Hebrew translation of the Greek title, Ecclesiastes. There are many reasons for the universal appeal of Qoheleth's poem. The images are simple and unadorned, but they capture the rhythm that is part of every person's experience. Some people are attracted by the way in which Qoheleth portrays the ebb and flow of life. They feel he has expressed something of its dignity and direction. Others discover in these lines a sense of consolation. They respond to what seems to be a quiet acceptance of the balance between joy and pain, life and death. An entire generation of Americans might associate these lines with the death of John F. Kennedy. It was one of his favorite passages and was read as part of his funeral liturgy. Still others have found a vitality in this poem that borders on optimism. During the more enthusiastic days of the peace movement, Pete Seeger put Qoheleth's words to music. The song became part of a growing belief that the times were indeed changing and that life could not only be different but even new.

What most people do not realize, however, is that Qoheleth's poem is neither accepting nor consoling. It is neither quiet nor optimistic. It is a cry for help. It is a desperate search for meaning in a world that seems devoid of all personal significance. Beneath the poetic symmetry and balanced images is a feeling of futility. Between the lines there are shadows and urgent questions. One need only read the poem in the context of the entire book to discover that Qoheleth is searching for the value of human life with the same intensity that a drowning man struggles for air. Qoheleth rejects all the usual answers to life's most vexing problems. His book is a radical critique of all the easy proverbs with which men have attempted to justify their lives. He demands more than excuses or intellectual subterfuges. This poem belongs to a man who is straining with all that is in him to find meaning in human life.

But he can find none.

In the end it is only his resigned faith in God which prevents Qoheleth from plunging into despair. His questions are so penetrating, his conclusions so sceptical that many scripture scholars have wondered how his writings ever became part of the canon of sacred scripture. But there is a reason for Qoheleth's place in the history of God's self-revelation. It is an extremely important reason for those of us who share the search for meaning in the last quarter of the 20th century. Most people find that the best way to handle difficult questions is not to ask them. They find ways of hiding from the painful side of life. Qoheleth, on the other hand, is one of a tradition of brave questioners. He dares to face the difficult questions about man and to pursue those issues beyond the limits of human understanding. Qoheleth was doing what Viktor Frankel, many centuries later, would do, in a Nazi death camp; what Pascal did in the dark night of his doubt; what Camus did in the face of absurdity. Qoheleth wrote for the same reason that Thoreau gave for going to Walden: he wanted to "drive life into a corner." He chose to weigh the human condition on the scales of suffering and death. Qoheleth was pushing life to the outer limits. He was trying to decide about hope.

Qoheleth has been aptly described as the existentialist of the Old Testament. He is a poet of human existence because he is close to life and feels deeply the longing that stirs within it. He strives to clothe human meaning in the language of the earth, for he knows that man, like the earth, has his seasons. These are the seasons of the soul—the inner weather of our existence where we know both the impenetrable night of doubt and the glimpse of dancing sunlight. There are the seasons of the self: the transitions, the storms and lulls within each of us. There is also the collective season of an age: the condition of soul of an entire culture or society.

Qoheleth saw this relationship between the seasons of the earth and the seasons of man's inner self. He found himself wondering whether this relationship held any significance for the destiny of man. When he studied the earth's seasons he found himself unable to go beyond the endless cycles of life and death, sowing and reaping, being born and dying. There was movement but it was forever folding back upon itself. His search into nature for a transcendent purpose led him nowhere. "There is nothing new under the sun," he says with finality (1:9). When he looks for meaning within the seasons of man's soul, Qoheleth encounters the same inexorable repetition. Man, too, is trapped in the wheel of birth and death. There is nothing new in the sunlight of human consciousness. The only thing different about man is that he hungers to make sense of it all and therefore experiences his quest as frustrating and laden with futility. Qoheleth's conclusion regarding human life and effort is as sceptical as his search into the rhythmic patterns of the earth. "What a weary task God has given mankind to labour at! I have seen everything that is done under the sun, and what vanity it all is, what chasing of the wind!" (1:13–14).

For Qoheleth "all is vanity." There is a season for everything but a meaning for nothing. There is a time for everything but a direction for nothing. The seasons of the earth and the seasons of man are not a journey toward meaning but a treadmill into oblivion. There is a season for everything except for hope.

It does not follow, however, that Qoheleth experiences life as a season of despair. Despair is inward death and Qoheleth is not dead inside. He is still questioning, still searching the horizon for signs of promise. It would be more correct to say that Qoheleth experiences life as a season of hunger. Despair is an emptiness, a void. Hunger is a cry from deep inside, a vacuum that longs to be filled. There is a difference between an empty pit and a desolate heart. Despair is an empty pit. Qoheleth is an aching, hungry spirit that is starved for meaning and for hope. Where there is hunger of spirit, no matter how frustrated or oppressed, there is still openness to hope. It would be a painful experience to awaken some morning and discover that there is no more bread. But what if one were to awaken and discover that he is no longer hungry? Where there is hunger there is still life.

Qoheleth is like a photographic negative of hope —his quest for light continues to appear in the form of darkness. The outlines of his life cry out to be seen under different light or from a new angle of vision. His writings end in a spiritual vacuum, but it is a vacuum shaped in the image of life. He cries out to be filled with the vision of hope.[1]

Where do we stand in relation to Qoheleth? What is the season of man's soul in the 20th century? How have the storms of history affected the inner weather of our vision?

The questioning voice of our time which most closely resembles that of Qoheleth belongs to the French writer, Albert Camus. In one of his essays entitled *Neither Victims Nor Executioners,* Camus attempts to portray the season of man's soul in this age: "The 17th century was the century of mathematics, the 18th that of the physical sciences, and the 19th that of biology. Our 20th century is the century of fear."[2]

Camus has uncovered the anxious underside of man's inner self. We are a people of many moods but beneath the surface of most of our lives there flows an undercurrent of fear. We stand in dread of our own powers. Because of the misuse of those powers we have known one side of Qoheleth's seasons with intensity. Ours has been a season of dying and uprooting, of killing and tearing down, of tears and mourning, of throwing away, of separation, of losing and tearing asunder, of speaking out, of hating, and of war. If we lived in the age of Qoheleth we could perhaps count on the inevitability of the cycles to bring us relief from our fears and from the seasons of destruction. If we lived in the age of Qoheleth we might be more willing to count on the simple rhythms of time to bring back the seasons of giving birth, of planting, of healing and building, of laughter and dancing, of loving and peace. Since the time of Qoheleth, however, the earth's seasons, together with the circle of life which surrounds man as his environment, have become far more dependent upon the choices of man than on the inevitable cycles of nature. Qoheleth could depend on the power of the earth to renew itself. Today we ourselves are faced with the awesome responsibility of caring for the earth and for the future of the human community. We have history on our hands.

Like Qoheleth, Camus searched to make sense of man. He also encountered the same dark enigma. But now the stakes were higher, the uneasiness deeper. Qoheleth's experience of vanity became Camus' encounter with absurdity, and without Qoheleth's tenuous link of faith in God, Camus moved from resignation to metaphysical rebellion. Like Qoheleth, Camus was willing to ask the hard questions and to pursue those questions to the outer limits. He too attempted to drive life into a corner. He rejected all forms of other-worldly hope as an escape from the call to be faithful to man and to the earth. Camus, like Qoheleth, was trying to decide about hope.

He decided against it.

But this is not to say that he decided for despair. The Nobel prize author died at the height of his literary and intellectual career in a tragic car accident. He carried a burning love for humanity and a restless, questioning heart to his grave. Camus' greatest concern was that man's fear might paralyze his questioning and his freedom. Of all our fears perhaps the most awesome is the possibility that we might give up inside. Millions have been killed by warfare in this century, but millions more have simply died inside. They have died from a heart failure that cannot be monitored on an electrocardiograph. They still walk around. They still perform all of the gestures and movements which we identify as human. But the fire inside of them has died. They have lost the vision. They have lost what Boris Pasternak calls "the inward music." They have lost both the hunger of Qoheleth and the rebellion of Camus. They are no longer trying to make sense even out of the absurd.

It isn't that we lack people who are willing to look into the future. We have an abundance of prophets, but they are for the most part prophets of doom. Much of the literature and art of our time has become apocalyptic; it expresses itself in the language of crisis and urgency. In books such as *1984* and *Brave New World*, in films such as *On The Beach* or *Soylent Green*, we are confronted again and again with impending disaster. The mirror of the future which is held up in the face of man today is a mirror of failure, a portrait of despair. We have no lack of predictions and forecasts, but we do lack a vision.

We are in urgent need of a reason to go on. "Without a vision," writes the author of Proverbs, "the people perish." Centuries ago Qoheleth had the courage to question. In our time Camus had the courage to rebel. Today we need more than questions and rebellion. We need a vision.

Where can we look for such a vision? Where can we find the inner resources to create a season of hope? If we who bear the name Christian believe what we say, the answer to this question is clear. The Christian gospel *is* the vision of hope. It is the promise of meaning for human life. More than that, it is the living way for man to discover and realize that promise. Christianity is the season of hope unfolding within the soul of man. Between Qoheleth and Camus there is Jesus.

But what of Jesus? And what of us who follow him? What are the loaves and fishes of meaning he gives us? And what are these among so many people who are starving for hope? What has he accomplished that is significant enough to elicit an unconditional response of trust from man? How has he brought purpose and direction into the seasons of the earth and of man's soul?

One possibility is that Jesus discovered a way of *escaping* from the tension of living and dying, of laughing and weeping. There are some religions and forms of thought which approach the human dilemma in this way. They attempt to solve the problem of being human by searching for a means of escape. To read the Christian gospel is to know that this is not the way of Christ. If being human is looked upon as a problem to be solved, then Jesus offers no solution. He only offers his life as a mystery of trust and love. Jesus did not look for a way to avoid the dark seasons of the soul. He offered no escape from the beauty or the burden of walking on the earth.

Like every other human being, Jesus experienced moments of exhilarating joy and wonder. He shared the beauty of the earth and of human friendship. He knew the weariness of physical labor, the irritation of sweat in his eyes, the beauty of sunsets and moonrises.

But, like every other human being, there were also times when Jesus drew back in fear from the darkness and the suffering. There were days when he wrestled in the desert of his inner self, when he sought the meaning of his mission and what it would cost him as a person. There were times when he wished it could have been otherwise—that the seasons of pain and loneliness, weariness and dying could be avoided.

The most striking instance of this occurred at the climax of his life. Jesus walked out of the supper room and into a garden. It was there in the garden that Jesus accomplished what Qoheleth had tried to do—he drove life into a corner and confronted the meaning of existence in its barest essentials. When he walked into Gethsemani, his deepest feeling was that of fear and the desire that the external circumstances of his life might be altered. The season of sorrow swept through him like a river. His inner self became heavy with dread. His prayer at that moment is the cry of all humanity in the face of pain: "Father, if it is possible, let this chalice pass me by." How many times has every human being voiced that prayer? Lord, let it be different. Please change it all. Please take away the pain.

In Matthew's account the agony of Christ becomes the encounter between the human desire to avoid suffering and the call of the Father to enter its terrifying depths with trust. This confrontation took place in the consciousness of Jesus with a wrenching intensity. Three times Jesus cried out for a means of escape. Three times he chose the way of trust. The breakthrough of hope came there in the garden. It came when the prayer for deliverance became the prayer of unconditional trust: "My father, if this cup cannot pass by without my drinking it, your will be done" (Mt 26:42). When Jesus walked out of the garden, none of the external circumstances had changed. The tragic events of his passion began to unfold immediately. On the outside nothing was different. But within, in the season of man's soul, everything had been transformed. The breakthrough to hope had occurred forever. The inward journey of Christ is the way to life for those who follow him. Externally speaking, faith in Jesus changes nothing. It offers no solutions for or escapes from the painful dimension of being human. Faith does not take away pain or the sheer grief of loss. There is still dying and mourning, crying out and searching. The weeds still grow among the wheat. Uprooting will follow the planting. Jesus challenges those who seek for hope to follow him on the same dark journey: "If anyone wants to be a follower of mine, let him renounce himself and take up his cross and follow me. For anyone who wants to save his life will lose it but anyone who loses his life for my sake will find it" (Mt 16:24–25).

Viewed from the outside the circumstances of a Christian's life are no easier or smoother than anyone else's. If Jesus' life and words are any indication, a Christian can expect more suffering rather than less. But beneath the surface flow of events, spring has burst forth. Inwardly, a Christian's life is radically transformed into the season of hope.

Like Qoheleth, Jesus spoke of the earth's seasons but he assures us that we can accept these cycles, not with skeptical resignation, but with trust. For within them and beneath them a new creation is coming to birth. That creation is a journey towards life. The kingdom—the season of hope—is here among us. Quietly but surely, like seeds in good earth, like yeast in dough, like a tiny mustard seed, the kingdom of God is growing. The parables of the kingdom were images of hope which Jesus employed to reassure his disciples that despite external appearances the kingdom of the Father was coming into the world. The Christian need only be like a farmer who cultivates the earth with confidence. He can give himself over to the earth's powers. When he trusts the Father enough to entrust his very self to the cycles of living and dying, then the season of hope has arrived within him.

Like Qoheleth, Jesus spoke of the seasons of man's soul. Unlike Qoheleth, he urged his followers

not only to read the earth's signs well but to be prepared for new signs—the signs of the planting, the
growing, and the coming to harvest of the kingdom
of God. "Take the fig tree as a parable: as soon as
its twigs grow supple and its leaves come out, you
know that summer is near. So with you, when you
see all these things: know that he is near, at the
very gates" (Mt 24:32–33).

Like many concerned prophets of today, Jesus
used the language of crisis and urgency. But there
is a striking difference in the way Jesus employs his
apocalyptic images. For him, crisis is not a disaster
but an opportunity. "When these things begin to
take place, stand erect, hold your heads high, because your liberation is near at hand" (Lk 21:28). A
Christian is one who believes that in the midst of
crisis he is summoned to stand tall and to walk with
confidence because he walks in the season of hope.

The message of Qoheleth, even in its skepticism,
appears to most people as common sense. It appears
to be common sense that there are good days and
bad days. It appears to be public knowledge that
man can do very little about changing the seasons
of the earth or of his soul. Hope, on the other hand,
comes as a surprise, as a contradiction to the world
of common sense. Perhaps that is why St. Paul refers
to hope as a mystery—a secret. Hope is God's secret
which he has shared with all men in the person of
Jesus. To be a Christian is to know the secret and
to share it: "I became the servant of the Church
when God made me responsible for delivering God's
message to you, the message which was a mystery

hidden for generations and centuries and has now been revealed to his saints. It was God's purpose to reveal it to them and to show all the rich glory of this mystery to the pagans. The mystery is Christ among you, your hope of glory" (Col 1:25–26).

The divine secret is that the enfleshment of God is the transformation of man. When we begin to understand the implications of this mystery, we will also recapture the compelling power of Christianity as a vision of hope. It is the basis for describing the story of Jesus as good news.

Qoheleth told us nothing startling or new about being human. He just said it poetically and with skeptical insight. Camus did not uncover a new dimension of man's nature or destiny; he simply looked with honesty at the experience of modern man. Through their poets and questioners men have been able to explore the feeling and fabric of what they experience as given and claim as obvious. There has always been the temptation to approach the human condition as though it were only a question of common sense. But the Christian demands that there is more to life than meets the eye of human realism. He claims that there is indeed something *new* under the sun. He believes that the world of common sense does not reveal the whole truth about man. "What for the pagans was small publicity," writes Chesterton, "is for the Christian a gigantic secret." It is small, insignificant and public knowledge that man's soul shares the same seasons as the earth. It is a gigantic secret that there is hope and eternal life within that struggle. It is old, worn out realism that man is wounded with suffering and fated with death. It is good news that because of Christ's life, death and resurrection, all of history is transformed into a new creation.

The Christian secret is unlike all other secrets: it is not intended to be kept. This is "good news of great joy for the whole people" (Lk 1:10). More than any technological discovery or scientific formula, men today are crying out for an inner vision, for a reason to go on. Perhaps at no other time in history has the world so desperately needed to know the secret of Christian hope. Unfortunately, this hope is often kept a well guarded secret within Christianity itself. The vision is often buried beneath the relics of a worn out or superstitious faith. Too often Christians have looked to hope as an escape hatch rather than a commitment. They have approached the Christian vision as a way out, rather than a way through. They have looked to Jesus to save them *from* the human condition instead of saving them *in* the human condition.

In the document concerning the role of the church in the modern world, the Second Vatican Council summons all Christians to "read the signs of our times." The Latin title of this document is *Gaudium et Spes*—"Joy and Hope." It is a call to understand the climate of man's soul in this age and to scan the horizon for signs of hope. It is a call to recognize the vision that is ours as Christians. It is an invitation to receive the loaves of hope which Jesus gives us, and which, through our sharing, can be multiplied to feed the human family. What the Christian has to bring to the last quarter of the 20th century is not blind optimism or an easy way out. He has no simple answers to the fears that flow through all of us. But he does have the secret. He has the gigantic secret of Christian hope. The Christian is summoned to announce by his life that the seasons of man's soul —the agony and ecstasy of being human are, in the end, the unfolding of the new creation. It is a time to be born. It is the season of hope. Ironically, a modern Christian might well take the haunting words of Camus as a description of his own experience: "In the midst of winter, I finally learned that there was in me an invincible summer."

Chapter Three

IT IS ENOUGH, LORD, LET ME DIE

The Crisis of Hope

There is a scene in the film, *Me, Natalie,* that suggests a starting point for a reflection on hope. Natalie knows that she is not a beautiful girl. When she is encouraged by her uncle to be more optimistic about herself, Natalie turns to him and asks: "What are you trying to do, give me hope?" "Would you like some hope?" her uncle responds. After a moment, she replies: "Hope, yes, but not lies."

We are sometimes tempted to approach the topic of hope with the wand of optimism. In an age other than ours, this might have been possible and even appropriate. But the clouds that move across our land are not wisps of promise. They are storm clouds, heavy with fear and anxiety. The air is charged with a strident note of realism. We have, in fact, become realistic to the point of being cynical. We are sober to the point of nearly losing our capacity to dream. Natalie is not alone these days. Our troubled age is seeking desperately for something to hope in, but it refuses adamantly to trust in illusions. Like Natalie, we are as fearful of lies as we are hungry for hope. Hope, yes, but not lies.

How can a Christian respond to the restless search of this age? What word of hope can a Christian speak with his life? The Second Vatican Council describes a Christian not as a distant spectator but as a participator in man's search for a meaningful future: "The joys and the hopes, the griefs and the anxieties of the men of this age, especially those who are poor or in any way afflicted, those, too, are the joys and hopes, the griefs and anxieties of the followers of Christ."[1] The Christian response to the crisis of hope is not an attitude of indifference. The Christian is not an "easy rider" who carefully skirts the chaotic forces of this age. "If God has become man," says Thomas Merton, "then no Christian is ever allowed to be indifferent to man's fate." A Christian begins the search for hope where all men must begin—by confronting the despair that threatens to engulf him. A Christian knows that the path to life is not a freeway. He knows that Christian hope is more than human optimism. He knows that blind optimism is just that—blind, blind to the jagged edges of life, as well as to the healing power of pain. He does not seek a cheap hope born of wishful thinking, but a resurrection hope born of real living and real dying.

It is not that a Christian is unaware of the music of life. He knows that fear needs to sing just as Zorba needs to dance. In that sense, the Christian carries in his heart a buoyancy that can aptly be described as optimism. But it is the quality and the direction of the song that sets Christian hope apart from the masquerade of blind optimism. If the Christian whistles in the dark, he does so while walking *into* the darkness, not away from it. His is a melody of transformation, not of escape. His hope can only be as real as the despair he wrestles to death. Perhaps that is why a Christian trusts that he will eventually find himself smiling through his tears.

Nowhere is this paradox that we call the passover mystery more evident than in the events of God's word. We are accustomed to look to scripture for consolation and confidence, but the Word of the Lord is not always comforting. Enfleshed as it is in the dark soil of the human condition, the Word of God is often disturbing, even unnerving. Sometimes it is a story of desperation. Yet it is this Word, born in struggle and transformed through painful growth, that summons man to a vision of hope which surpasses the darkest canyons of his despair.

There is a story about the near despair of a man of God. Not just any man of God, but a prophet—a man we would expect to be on fire with a vision of hope. If we would reflect on man's struggle for hope today, we might consider the desperation of a man named Elijah: "When Ahab told Jezebel all that Elijah had done and how he had put all the prophets to the sword, Jezebel sent a messenger to Elijah to say: 'May the gods do this to me, and more, if, by this time tomorrow, I have not made your life like the life of one of them!' He was afraid and fled for his life. He came to Beersheba, a town of Judah, where he left his servant. He himself went on to the wilderness, a day's journey, and sitting under a furze bush, wished he were dead. 'Yahweh,' he said, 'I have had enough. Take my life . . .' " (I Kgs 19: 1–4).

There are many times of drama in a prophet's life: the fiery days of courage, the moments of confrontation and triumph, the long months of waiting and watching. Elijah lived all of these fully. He was, after all, the primordial prophet, the beginning of a long tradition of holy men which would culminate in Jesus. Elijah strode through days when his courage blazed out like the desert sun. He tasted victory over the false prophets of Baal with a confidence that bordered on arrogance. Why else would he have poured buckets of water over the altar before calling upon Yahweh to set it ablaze? Like most of the prophets, Elijah spent many of his days in trouble. We expect prophets to be in trouble, but we are not used to seeing them in flight. We certainly do not expect them to give up under a desert bush and ask to die.

There are many moments in a prophet's life, but we are interested in Elijah at *this* moment. We are interested in Elijah in flight, Elijah in fear, Elijah crying out against the wasteland. There is something we recognize in Elijah at this moment; a kinship of feeling, an expression on his face. Elijah has just confronted the religious and moral chaos of his times in the persons of Ahab and Jezebel. The result this time is not victory but flight into the desert. Suddenly Elijah the prophet can neither see into the future nor understand the present. At this moment, he is neither a man of vision nor a man who confronts. He is a man in flight, glancing over his shoulder at the upheaval of his age, peering with blinded eyes into the wasteland of the future. He does not appear to be a true prophet. He could be any frightened human figure, wandering Cain-like across the face of the earth. He could be Updike's Rabbit on the run. He could be Vonnegut's Billy Pilgrim. He could be you. He could be me.

We are interested in Elijah at this moment when his stark and lonely figure could be part of a film report for the evening news. Like Elijah, we find ourselves in a time of transition and flight. Glancing over our shoulders, we see the easy promises of the fifties breaking up on the rocks of the sixties and seventies. Suddenly, we are here together in the wasteland, confused by our miscalculations and frightened by our responsibilities. Bye Bye, American Pie. And the flag. And motherhood. And Uncle Sam. Twentieth century man is like a surveyor who begins by measuring his future for hope and ends by staking it out for despair. For the first time in 30,000 years, says the historian Arnold Toynbee, man is again using the word "survival" with deadly seriousness. The very instruments of our technological prowess now threaten us with self-destruction. Do we have computers or do they have us? We are no longer sure. Perhaps no previous generation has had to ask these questions with such urgency: Does man have a future? Is there anything worth hoping for? Is there something that we can live for?

There is an ancient biblical tradition that the courage of Elijah would come back to earth, and many felt that his prophetic fire had indeed returned in the person of John the Baptist. We know of no tradition that expected the *desperation* of Elijah to return. But it is here, with all of its anguish and loneliness. We catch glimpses of it in the eyes that meet ours in elevators and waiting rooms. We find mirrored there the reflections of our own fears. Together with Elijah, we are afraid. We are afraid that we might stop hoping. We are afraid that we might stop hungering enough inside to trust in someone beyond the margins of our own experience. We are afraid that we might allow the gift of our inwardness to be externalized into data banks.

Teilhard de Chardin has sometimes been described as a blind optimist. He is a man of hope, but not a mere optimist. In many ways, his exiled figure resembles that of Elijah. Teilhard describes his own deep apprehension in the oft quoted image of the card game: "We are the players as well as being the cards and the stakes. Nothing can go on if we leave the table. Neither can any power force us to remain. . . . If faced by the work involved we can say: 'What's the good of it all?' Our efforts will flag. With that the whole of evolution will come to a halt—because we are evolution."[2]

The greatest danger is not that we would begin doubting, but that we might stop trying. The greatest danger is that we might leave the table. "It is enough, Lord, let me die."

Elijah became a man in flight at the very moment

when he seemed to be most in charge of the situation. The crisis in our self-confidence has swept over us at the high point of our scientific development. It took man over two million years to go from the use of smooth rock tools to the use of chipped, sharp instruments. It has taken man less than seventy years to go from the sands of Kitty Hawk to the craters of the moon. And yet, it is at this moment that our confidence is most shaken.

Many contemporary thinkers have recognized the strange irony of this situation. Beneath the sense of confusion is an unspoken question which the poet Archibald MacLeish has effectively put into words: "And yet we cannot help but wonder why—why the belief in man has foundered; why it has foundered *now*—precisely *now*—now at the moment of our greatest intellectual triumphs, our never equaled technological mastery, our electronic miracles. Why was man a wonder to the Greeks—to Sophocles of all the Greeks—when he could do little more than work a ship to windward, ride a horse, and plow the earth, while now that he knows the whole of modern science he is a wonder to no one—certainly not to Sophocles' successors and least of all, in any case, to himself?"[3]

There are many possible answers to this question. The real issue, however, is not why man is facing a crisis in his self-confidence, but how he can respond creatively to the future. MacLeish's answer is that man must begin believing in man again. Along with many other dedicated humanists he calls for "the revolt of the diminished man"—a return to global self-confidence as the reality upon which a new age can be built. A Christian is also a humanist, but his search for hope is not limited to human endeavor. A Christian is a humanist with a transcendent perspective. He believes that the meaning of man can never be adequately grasped apart from man's relationship with the living God. For a Christian, faith in man is grounded upon hope in God. History is deeper than the story of man's quest to believe in himself.

If the story of Elijah had been only a story about man, it might have ended there in the desert under the bush. If the story of the 20th century were only a story about man, it might end on the outskirts of oblivion. But neither Elijah nor we are writing our stories alone. In the end, the first book of Kings is not so much a story of Elijah, the desperate prophet, as it is the story of Yahweh, the faithful God. God's fidelity is not shown by his taking over for man, or by working miracles. God is faithful to us by prodding us to fidelity to ourselves and to the present moment. Hope is God turning man's desperation into a search for a life direction: "Then he (Elijah) lay down and went to sleep. But an angel touched him and said, 'Get up and eat.' He looked round and there at his head was a scone baked on hot stones, and a jar of water. He ate and drank and then lay down again. But the angel of Yahweh came back a second time and touched him and said, 'Get up and eat, or the journey will be too long for you.' So, he got up and ate and drank, and strengthened by that food, he walked forty days and forty nights until he reached Horeb, the Mountain of God" (I Kgs 19: 5–8).

Elijah might give up on life, but Yahweh refused to give up on Elijah. There is a hint of playfulness in a God who prods his servant into wakefulness and, finally, into movement. What do you do with a God who refuses to let you alone? What do you say to a God whose love is stronger than your despair, whose summons is more persistent than your own self-pity? There are no words. Only that stirring from the very depths of your inner self. It is true, isn't it? If it were not for the Lord of life, we might long since have chosen death. And now quietly, but deliberately, we are walking.

In the end, hope does not come from man, not even from a holy man. In the end, hope comes from the living God who summons man out of the pit of his despair. Not all of the wishful thinking in the world can get a holy man across the desert. Not all the technology in the world can build us a city of peace if we do not have the heart to keep on walking.

The Christian today knows what Elijah felt. He knows that he has no secret formula to stifle the fears that surface all around him, for they are his own fears. What, then, does a Christian have to offer? He has the openness of heart not to give up on the prodding of God. He is open to being surprised by God. He is not willing to say it is forever finished, even when he feels that way inside. "Hope," says Gabriel Marcel, "is the radical refusal to set limits."

Elijah knew his own dark discouragement. He knew he could not rely on his own ingenuity, but he was still radically open to being moved by Yahweh. Hope is this radical openness to God. Hope is God transforming our flight into journey, our aimless wandering into a pilgrimage toward life.

It is not by accident that a theology of hope has emerged in the wake of the death of God movement. We are aware of a change in the way we experience and describe our world. Part of that change involves the collapse of notions that describe God as though he were "up there" or "out there." In reality, God has not died, even though our understanding of him has undergone a profound cultural upheaval. One of the reasons for our hope is that what appeared to be a collapse of the superstructure of faith has, in fact, been a deeper incarnation of God into the heart of history and into the heart of man. The God of "up there" and "out there" has become the "within" of man. In this way God has also become the "ahead" of man. Gregory Baum speaks of it as the transition from God the outsider, to God the insider. God has become the summons from within life to keep on going—the prodding, challenging presence, the call to leave the past behind and to create a new future. Elijah was desperate enough to want to die, but he was open enough to be called back into hope. "Remember, pilgrim," a Latin-American poet has written, "there is no road. The road is made by walking." Hope is made by walking. Hope is the journey itself and the destiny which is within man.

The question for our time, then, is not whether we can count on man, or even on one another, but whether we are willing to count on God who, in turn, counts on us. God is the light within us that refuses to be overcome by the darkness. God, as the theologians of hope are fond of saying, is the future of man. God is the future of man because his Spirit is the fire within us. God is the future of man because he stirs the embers beneath the ashes of our despair, because he prods us gently but persistently out of our self-pity.

Chapter Four

WERE NOT OUR HEARTS BURNING?

Hope and Expectancy

That same day two of them were on their way
to a village called Emmaus, which lay about
seven miles from Jerusalem, and they were
talking together about all these happenings.
As they talked and discussed it with one
another, Jesus himself came up and walked
along with them; but something held their eyes
from seeing who it was. He asked them,
'What is it you are debating as you walk?'
They halted, their faces full of gloom and
one, called Cleopas, answered, 'Are you the
only person staying in Jerusalem not to know
what has happened there in the last few days?'
'What do you mean?' he said. 'All this about
Jesus of Nazareth,' they replied, 'a prophet
powerful in speech and action before God and
the whole people; how our chief priests and
rulers handed him over to be sentenced to
death, and crucified him. But we had been
hoping that he was the man to liberate Israel. . . .
—Lk 24:13–21 *New English Bible*

The way to Emmaus is more than a road; it is an
experience in human life. It is more than an outward

47

change of scene; it is an inward transformation of self. There are times in all of our lives when the road we walk begins to take on the same landmarks of disillusionment. There are times when the two disciples become like old and familiar companions. The reasons for this are not to be found in a travel guide. What is at stake is not a change in physical location but a process of soul. It is not the seven miles from Jerusalem to Emmaus but the inner pilgrimage which brings Cleopas and his companion close to us. The journey to Emmaus is an experience in the landscape of the heart. It is an encounter with the hills and valleys of hope and despair. The road to Emmaus is a path that twists its way through fallen expectations and shattered dreams in search of new life. At various times and stages in our personal journey we become familiar with its terrain. It comes upon us whenever the outer circumstances of our lives call into question the inner reason for going on. Perhaps it is a personal goal that we never realized, a marriage that didn't last, a life that is fragmented, a profession that has become empty, a son or daughter who is alienated, an unexpected illness or a sudden death. Whatever the reasons for our disappointment, the outcome is the same. We find ourselves walking with the same heaviness of heart that the two disciples experienced. Perhaps we even find ourselves repeating the same haunting words. We had been hoping. . . .

The story of Emmaus has implications that go beyond the level of personal reflection. It is more than a description of individual experience. Today it is also the story of the church and of the world in which we live. It is the landscape of our culture, the pathway of contemporary history. It is the journey of the human race in our time. Within the Catholic Church, for example, one can discern the terrain of Emmaus in the road which leads from Vatican II to the present. There are the same landmarks of experience—the fallen expectations, the geography of bewilderment, the debates along the way, the faces full of gloom, the voices heavy with sadness. Many in the Christian community find themselves anxiously exploring what Daniel Berrigan calls "the geography of faith"—that desperate search to relocate the roots of our belief and the reason for our hope. The journey of Cleopas and his friend provides us with an important focus for our experience and reflection. It challenges us to explore the ways in which men today confront their disillusionment and despair.

What is most striking about these two men? How is their journey like ours? Where does the road to Emmaus lead us today?

What stands out most clearly is that the two disciples are speaking of hope in the past tense. We *had* been hoping. . . . Once there had been a vision; once their hearts had burned with newness and promise; once there had been crowds and miracles and stirrings among the common people; once all the signposts pointed toward Jerusalem and the coming of the kingdom. Now there is only the road to Emmaus.

When men begin to speak of hope in the past tense, it has already become the language of despair. Hope can only create the future if it is willing to commit itself to the present. When men consign their lives to the past, they barter tomorrow's promises for yesterday's expectations. It is only possible to say yes to tomorrow if we are willing to say yes to today. Past expectations cannot be the basis for tomorrow's hope. The past is gone. We can remember it with gratitude, we can flee from it with regret, or long for it with nostalgia; but we cannot hope in it or create the future out of it. We are given only the present with which to shape the future. The present is not the goal of our hope, nor is it the end of our hope, but it is the beginning of our hope. If we cannot face life as it is, we will never be able to shape it into what we feel it ought to be. "Now" is the adverb of Christian hope; it is the only available moment of choice and commitment. "Now is the favorable time," writes St. Paul," this is the day of salvation" (II Cor 6:2). Salvation is as near as this moment which pulses like a heartbeat through our lives. Every now is sacred because God has chosen to take time seriously. Through the incarnation of Christ the living God entered into the stream of history. He became the still point of all our moments. When God chose to encounter man at a certain moment in a certain place, he transformed the meaning and direction of time. No longer is it simply the treadmill of the seasons or the cycles of the planets. Time has become the adventure of sacred history. The companionship of man with God is inextricably bound to the unfolding of this history. Thus, man's quest for a meaningful future can only be realized if he is willing to seek the treasure buried in the soil of this moment and stake everything on it. To hope is to listen with one's heart and to respond with one's life in *this* moment and at *this* time.

Faced with a painful and bewildering present, the two disciples allowed their hope to slip into the past. Because they spoke of hope from the ruins of their past expectations, they missed the call to life hidden in the fabric of the present moment. They were so disillusioned with what they thought Jesus should have been that they missed the person he had actually become. The reality of the present far transcended their limited political plans, but they were blinded to the new creation which even now was emerging from the ruins of their shattered dreams.

When men begin to speak of hope in the past tense they also begin to speak of God as though he were absent. Along the highway of despair God is only a stranger that we meet but do not recognize. Luke says that something prevented the two disciples from recognizing Jesus. What was that something? Was it something in the appearance or attitude of Jesus? Was he disguising his true identity? However mysterious the post-resurrection appearances were, it is clear that what prevented his followers from recognizing Jesus was not a disguise on his part, but an attitude on the part of those whom he encountered. Because the two disciples walked with backward glances they were not prepared to see Jesus walking alongside of them. The something which prevented them from recognizing

Jesus was their failure to trust in the present and to embrace the Emmaus road as the pathway to a new future. When hope dies in the present, God becomes a stranger out of the past. God is always an alien in the land of despair.

There are many ways that we have allowed God to become a stranger in our time. Abraham Heschel, writing from the tragic perspective of Auschwitz and Buchenwald, says that the characteristic religious experience of contemporary man is that of the *absence* of God. His words are echoed in the writings of the theologians who speak of the death of God as an event in our history. This experience of what Martin Buber refers to as "the eclipse of God" is part of the landscape and the terrain of the contemporary journey toward Emmaus. There is little doubt that many people experience God as absent from their lives. There are many theoretical atheists today, but there are far more practical atheists, who, whatever they might think about God's existence, have not allowed him to draw near enough to make a difference in their lives. The question therefore remains: Is God absent from us, or are we somehow absent from him as he continues to journey at our side?

There is another way of looking at the same question. The experience of the absence of God is not the same as the experience of despair. It could be an invitation to hope. To feel someone's absence is to miss that person. It is a sign that we long for the presence of the person who is apart from us. We say that absence makes the heart grow fonder. Perhaps what we really mean is that absence makes the heart grow more hungry. Hunger is the doorway to hope. Absence can make the heart more expansive with yearning and longing. In this sense, the experience of the absence of God may be one of the most significant summons to hope in our lives. It is a call to look for him in the present, to search for him among the strangers, to be open to the surprises of his divine love.

If we are willing to entrust ourselves to the present, we will have made the first step toward rediscovering the sacred. We will become open once again to enter into dialogue with the God who walks with us as man, and who takes on our darkness and our death in order to give us new life. If we are willing to entrust ourselves to the present, even if that road resembles the terrain from Jerusalem to Emmaus, we will have opened ourselves to the possibility of resurrection in the face of death.

The quality of feeling that accompanies this commitment to the present is best described as the spirit of expectancy. To be a Christian is to expect great things to happen. It is to expect newness and surprise. It is to be always ready to find new skins for the wine of the gospel. It is to live in constant readiness, knowing that the definitive event of history is already under way. That event is the passover journey of Jesus—his life, death and resurrection. In that journey the breakthrough to life has irrevocably occurred. Now every moment is a *kairos*—an opportune time, a straining forward of the whole universe toward its fulfillment. There is something in the wind. More correctly, there is *someone* in the wind: the Spirit of Jesus, who has become the life breath of every moment, the divine wind that moves over the chaotic waters of every age.

There is an important difference between living in the spirit of expectancy and living with a set of expectations. Expectations are projections of our private wishes and needs. Expectations are the prefabricated plans that become the conditions which we impose on the future. The spirit of expectancy, on the other hand, is a stance of openness, an unconditional gesture of trust toward the adventure at the heart of life. A set of expectations is at best a selective openness, and at worst a fearful barrier to the future. To demand the future on our terms is to lose the future as a life-giving process. Expectations are subtle but effective ways of removing the element of risk from life. Man needs risk to allow his freedom to become creative. Risk is the soil in which the seed of hope must die in order to bring forth new life. Expectations are futile attempts to bypass this dark soil of risk. When we plant the seed of the future in the shallow soil of expectations, we doom the seed to certain death.

The two disciples had imposed a set of expectations on Jesus. "We had been hoping that he was the man to liberate Israel," they told the stranger. Jesus had indeed liberated Israel, but the narrow and confining expectations of what liberation meant to them blinded these two men to anything greater. They were not prepared for a liberation of such radical dimensions as the resurrection. Their expectations had paralyzed their spirit of expectancy.

In our time we have experienced the tension between the call to live in the spirit of expectancy and the temptation to depend on our expectations. This has been at once the century of great expectations and the age of great disillusionment. Both in society and in the Christian community we have too easily substituted our private plans for a spirit of genuine openness to the power of God. We had been hoping. . . . We had been hoping that this was to be man's coming of age. We had been hoping that a new era of human progress was about to begin. But we were deceived. The age of Aquarius has not arrived. The greening of America did not happen. Flower power has wilted. The structures of government are in crisis on all levels. Technology threatens to become a Pandora's box. Our energy resources have become critical. In the face of so many fallen expectations there is a feeling of futility which pervades the land. The road signs all point toward Emmaus.

The church is the extension of Christ in space and time. Joined with the members of his risen body, Jesus stands at the axis of every age. He is, as T. S. Eliot puts it, "the still point of the turning world." Because the church is enfleshed in history, it has experienced the shock waves of change which have swept like an earthquake through all levels of our society. The church has been part of this age of great expectations. Together with the rest of our future-shocked culture, it is now experiencing withdrawal symptoms. Unfortunately, many in the church approached the renewal with the same naive optimism which characterized the stance of 20th century man towards his scientific progress. We expected great changes but we were not prepared for great crisis. We were not prepared for confusion or for the agony of a polarized church. We were not prepared for faith itself to be thrown into doubt. We were not prepared to be disappointed in our expectations for the future. We were, in short, not prepared to walk the road to Emmaus.

Those who looked to the church as a haven of security in the midst of social upheaval have been bitterly disappointed. Together with the rest of humanity, we have found our expectations badly shaken. We wrestle with unanswered questions and grope in the dark for a way through the maze of our bewilderment. What has happened to the church? Is this renewal or collapse? Have we updated the church or lost touch with the tradition of faith? It is not only in the world of science and technology that one hears the words of Cleopas and his friend. They are echoed in many places in the Christian community. We had been hoping . . . . We had been hoping that the renewal in the church would be a second Pentecost. We had been hoping for a transformation similar to that which occurred when the first disciples broke out of their locked doors and began to turn the world upside down. We had been hoping that new forms of liturgy would generate parish communities which would be alive with the Spirit. We had been hoping that the rediscovery of the church's mission to the world would call forth an increase of vocations to the ministry and to religious life. We had been hoping that new structures of leadership would provide the basis for shared responsibility.

But our hopes have fallen short. We find ourselves surrounded with plans that are not realized and projects that are left unfinished. Along with the two disciples we have allowed the spirit of expectancy to be reduced to a series of expectations. We have confused the spirit of Christian hope with planning for security. In doing so, we have been confronted again with the central paradox of the gospel—new birth is neither simple nor easy. No person or community of persons can be renewed without the pain of uncertainty and death. Hope is a commitment to the present with its ambiguity and its crucifixion.

Like the two disciples, it would be easy for us to spend the next several years looking back upon an age which seemed far more secure and comfortable than ours. It would be easy for us to weep over "bare ruined choirs." There are many Christians who would like to turn back the clock of history. They would like to be free from the uncertainty of this hour. But that is not the form of freedom the gospel demands of us. "It's a disgrace to be free of your age," writes the Russian poet, Yevtushenko, "a hundred times more shameful than to be its slave." To live in the past might provide a wistful sense of nostalgia, but it will not move the church into the future. The church is in need of Christians who are willing to commit themselves to the present struggle rather than to cling to their past expectations. The future belongs to those who are willing to recognize the face of Christ along the road of this age. It belongs to those who are willing to hear his question: "Was it not ordained that Christ should suffer and so enter into his glory?" Is it not necessary that the church experience suffering and uncertainty in order to be renewed?

We are encountering again the polarity between the gospel and life. We are learning that growth comes only through self-emptying. We are learning that there can be no rebirth without a death. We are a people who are learning how to hope. We are learning that hope is a verb before it is a noun, a direction of life rather than a state of mind, a freely chosen stance, rather than a trait of personality. A person might be born optimistic, but he must choose to be a man of hope. He may be buoyant by nature, but he becomes hopeful only through a radical commitment.

The journey to Emmaus begins in disillusionment and ends in recognition. It begins in bewilderment and ends in understanding. We remember Emmaus today not for its gloomy faces but for its burning hearts. We read the story of Emmaus because we believe that our journey will not end on the road of despair but at the table of hope. We listen to the account of the two disciples to remind ourselves not to look for Jesus among the dead, but to seek for him among the living. He has gone before us into Galilee. He is to be found in the marketplace of life.

The Christian believes that the collapse of his expectations is an invitation to rediscover the spirit of expectancy. It is a call to hear in the sounds of struggle which are all around us, not the rattle of death, but the pangs of birth. The task of the Christian in our time is to listen to the stranger who joins us on the road and to walk with him. If we ask him, he will stay with us. He will break bread with us and we will recognize him. Recognition is the eye of hope. It is the light that dawns after a long night, the sun that rises in our hearts. Recognition is more than a mere grasping of facts. It is an encounter with a person. The biblical meaning of knowledge always implies this intimate sharing of life. We will *know* the Lord in the act of sharing bread and journey. In knowing him we will also recognize one another. In the words of Teilhard, "Christ binds us and reveals us to one another."

We will recognize him in the *breaking*—the breaking up of old expectations and false securities, the breaking up of closed minds and narrow horizons, the destruction of death to make room for new life.

We will recognize him in the breaking of the *bread*. Bread is the substance of life and sharing. It is a symbol of hope. Bread is the form hope takes in order to nourish us. Broken in an act that looks like destruction, it is eaten in an act that looks like sharing. In the breaking up of expectations we lose our foothold in the world of security. In the sharing of our brokenness, we rediscover that we are brothers and sisters. We rediscover that the church is more than its structures, that the Spirit cannot be confined, that God's ways are more powerful than the plans of men. Along the road of despair we were, at best, suspicious colleagues. At the table of hope we become true companions. The word "companion" comes from the Latin: *cum* (with) and *panis* (bread). A companion is one who shares the bread of life with us. He shares the breaking up of the past in order to participate in the creation of a new future. A companion is one who joins us in celebrating life as a banquet of hope.

Tomorrow. Perhaps tomorrow, as we look back on these years of uncertainty, we will recall that the stranger has been walking with us all along the road. We will remember that even when the confusion was greatest, when he seemed most a stranger, even then our hearts were burning within us. That fire is the same fire as the hunger which led Elijah to eat and Qoheleth to search. It is the unquenchable fire of hope. "Men do not die from the darkness," says Miguel De Unamuno, "they die from the cold." It is not our doubts, not our confusions, not the darkness that could destroy us. It is the cold—the cold of despair if we give up, or the cold of our isolation if we choose to walk alone. Our confusion and our heaviness can be shared with others. Our pain can become wheat for the bread of recognition. It can be ground into flour for the bread of hope. At the table, when this bread is broken, we will remember the road again. But we will see it in a new way. And like the two disciples we will ask a new question: Were not our hearts burning within us as he spoke with us on the way?

Chapter Five

GIVE ENCOURAGEMENT
TO EACH OTHER

Hope and Relationships

I once met a man whose hope survived the death of his dreams. His name was Tsei Hu. He had been sent by the Nationalist Chinese government to the United States to study international law and diplomacy. As a young military officer, he had a promising political career ahead of him. When I first met Tsei Hu, however, he was in a hospital in Washington, D.C. His dreams for the future had come to an end in an automobile accident which left him a helpless quadraplegic abandoned by his government and alone in a strange land.

Tsei Hu was a Christian by birth. In the hospital he came near enough to despair to become a Christian by choice. He was not a model sufferer. I am quite certain that he will never be declared a saint. Perhaps that is why I was attracted to him. I could imagine myself responding to the situation in a similar fashion. I was drawn to him in his humanness, but I was frightened by his pain. I dreaded visiting him, because I knew he would confront me with all the questions about suffering that have no answers. Tsei knew that he was incurable. He also knew that he was dying a slow, inevitable death. I went to visit him once a week. I would write letters for him and we'd talk about Christianity. It was during those months that I learned about the power and the poverty of human words. I learned that there are no easy phrases in the face of suffering.

One day when I stopped to see Tsei, I found him depressed and in pain. I tried to talk but he remained sullen and silent. Feeling increasingly desperate, I bent near him and said: "You're not giving up, are you, Tsei? You're not going to stop hoping, are you?" Without looking at me, he responded bluntly: "There isn't anything left to hope in." I felt hollow inside. Then he went on: "But I still trust in God." Finally he looked at me, smiled weakly, and said: "And I still trust you. . . ."

A few months later Tsei Hu died. He never knew how deeply he touched my life that day. As usual, I could not find the words to tell him. It is only in the years since then that I have become aware of how much he gave me in that bedside encounter. He gave me the gift of understanding and trust. He gave me a glimpse of the gentleness of life even in its darkest moments. More than that, he gave me a new understanding of hope. Perhaps I can even find the words now to describe it.

Men hope for many things. They hope for their dreams to come true and for their plans to materialize. They hope for good fortune, for riches and recognition, for good health and long life. Tsei Hu was a man who, like all the rest of us, hoped for things. When he woke up immobilized on a hospital bed, he knew that more than his body had been shattered. He knew that his dreams were gone. He stared at the ceiling and saw despair written all over it. I do not know how he saw past that writing. But he did. I believe it had something to do with the Christian vision which he clung to desperately even as he complained about it. He suddenly found his life and his vision pushed beyond the threshold of things. Tsei Hu was challenged to go beyond his plans and dreams, beyond the fantasy of success and the trappings of his career, to seek out the value of life itself.

Tsei Hu taught me that the object of hope is not an object at all, but a person. I learned at his bedside that understanding is deeper than words. I learned that the goal of hope is not the things we hope for but the persons we trust in—the person of God and the human persons who image him. Just as faith is forced to go beyond the acceptance of formulas to become a commitment to a person, so hope is purified in the furnace of suffering to become trust in others. When hope is transformed into a personal bond, it becomes a new reality. We even give it a new name. We call it trust. Trust is hope in relationship.

How does anyone learn that trust is the real word for hope? Most of us have to learn it the hard way. We discover that what we think we are looking for, really is not it at all. We learn only painfully that we cannot find happiness in things or circumstances.

We are plagued by a hunger deep inside that says: there must be more; this cannot be all there is. It takes more than human wisdom to know that what we are hungry for is not the more of things, not the more of security and success, or of recognition. It takes the leap of faith to discover that the only things we ever keep are those we give away. It takes the vision of love to know that the truest form of hope is the trust we accept and the trust we give back to others.

Where does trust begin? Do we begin by trusting ourselves or by trusting others? Must we first experience the unconditional acceptance of others before we can begin to trust our own lives? Do we trust God first and then others, or do we experience his acceptance through the warmth of other human persons?

There is no simple answer to these questions. You cannot ask a circle of life where it begins. It will only speak of beginnings and ends at its center. Trust is such a circle of life. Whether it begins within us or outside of us is not the point. What is the point is that it begins only in relationships. We can reflect on the dimensions of trust only if we remember that they live in communion.

One part of the circle of life is the call to trust ourselves. Self-acceptance is the earth out of which all other forms of trust must grow. Whether or not we are able to trust another is dependent upon how well we trust the current of life that moves within us. There are no dreams without the dreamer, no plans without the planner, no bond of love without the pulse of trust in one's own heart. There can be no trust of others if we do not trust ourselves.

To dream dreams, to make plans, to reach out in love and trust requires self-confidence. We are often uneasy with the notion of self-confidence. In the past it was sometimes wrongly associated with the sin of pride. This misconception, in turn, distorted the meaning of humility. The humble man became the one who took a stance of self-deprecation. It is difficult to see anything virtuous in such an attitude. "The only thing the meek inherit," says Mordred, in *Camelot*, "is the dirt." The gospels, on the other hand, identify humility with trust in God *and* in one's self. Jesus describes self-confidence as a means of praising the Father: "You are the light of the world. A city built on a hill top cannot be hidden. No one lights a lamp to put it under a tub; they put it on the lamp stand where it shines for everyone in the house. In the same way, your light must shine in the sight of men so that seeing your good works they may give the praise to your father in heaven" (Mt 5:14–16).

To trust one's self is not an act of arrogance but a gesture of humility. The sin of pride is usually interpreted as the attitude of life which results from thinking one's self better than he is. The truth is, most of us suffer from the opposite affliction: we tend to think less of ourselves than we actually are. What we call pride—putting on airs or assuming roles is, more often than not, a gesture of fear and insecurity, a refusal to accept the gift that has been given us. It is an attempt to be someone else than who we really are. It is the self-defeating act of measuring ourselves by the gifts of others or of rooting our identity in things or circumstances outside of us. Our desperate attempts to avoid the truth of our lives are, in the end, futile. The flames of suffering, of disappointment and of disillusionment melt our masks and destroy our walls. When our roles and preoccupations are all stripped away, we are, like Tsei Hu, left only with ourselves and the fragile gift of life that is in our keeping. At that moment, when we think we have nothing left, we have, in fact, arrived at the core of life. *That* is the moment of truth. That is the moment of humility. It is also the moment of humanity, for their roots are the same. Humility and humanity both come from the same word—*humus*, i.e., the earth. A humble man is one who trusts his humanity because he loves the earth from which he came and upon which he walks. This is the moment of truth because it is a time of liberation from false expectations and roles. It is the opportunity to be truly ourselves. It is the moment of truth because it is a time to discover that we are more resilient than our roles, greater than our words, deeper than our despair; that we are more than our song, more even than our suffering and our doubts. We are *gift*. We are gift because we are given by the Lord, freely and lovingly. Trusting ourselves means nothing less than receiving joyfully the gift that God has shared with us.

John Berryman, the poet whose life was a grappling with despair, nevertheless had his moments of trust. In one of his "Eleven Addresses to the Lord," he has created a song of personal trust and praise:

> Master of beauty, craftsman of the snowflake,
> inimitable contriver,
> endower of earth so gorgeous and different from the
>   boring moon,
> thank you for such as it is my gift.[1]

To know God as the master of beauty is to accept a spark of that beauty in one's self. To experience him as craftsman of the snowflake is to love him as the artisan of man. To praise him as the inimitable contriver is to trust the surprise that is at the heart of all that is.

The gifts of God are gratuitous surprises. They confront us with a simple choice: we must accept them or reject them. There is no middle ground of human bargaining or self-justification. God's gifts cannot be earned or taken out in installments. There is nothing to mortgage, no down payments, no fine print, no legal forms, no consumer protection clauses, no lay-away plans, no C.O.D. The freest and most surprising of God's gifts is our own self-hood. The gift of self, above all, cannot be justified or earned. It can only be received. The first act of gratitude is the act of receiving. To say thank you is not to render a courtesy—it is to celebrate the gift for its own sake. Gratitude is an act of praise, not a social amenity.

When Tsei Hu told me that he trusted God, he was proclaiming quietly but firmly that he experienced his life as *gift*. From a human point of view, he appeared to have lost all the gifts that mattered—his status, his career, his possessions, his health. All things being equal, he should have been reduced to despair. The doctors declared him incurable. The nurses waited for him to die. But all things are not equal. Tsei Hu's life was not weighed out on human scales. From the perspective of Christian hope, his reduction to despair was actually a rediscovery of trust, a rewinning of his selfhood. Tsei had found the pearl of great price hidden in the field of human distractions. He could afford to let go of everything else in order to receive his life again. The person who has discovered the gift quality of his life is already a man of trust. He can then become a man of purpose and decision. He achieves what Jesus calls purity of heart.

The man who trusts his life has also discovered what Paul Tillich calls "the courage to be." Courage is a vital force that arises from the depth of the human heart. That is, in fact, its etymological root: *cor* (heart) and *agere* (to act). Courage is the power to act from the heart, from one's deepest self. A courageous man is one who risks his life because he trusts his gift.

There is a series of stories which Jesus used to illustrate this theme of risk. They include the parable of the talents and the story of the wise and foolish virgins (cf. Mt 25:1–30). Jesus tells these stories when he himself is about to risk his life for other men. He exhorts his followers to wait for his return in a spirit of watchfulness. But what does it mean to wait? What does it mean to watch? Jesus tells these stories to assure his followers that waiting and watching are not attitudes of passivity. To wait is to trust life enough to go into action. To watch is to move from the stance of a spectator to the response of a participator. In other words, Jesus challenges his followers to trust their gifts enough to risk them, to barter with them in the marketplace of life. The man who trusts his life will be willing to gamble it. He will dare to give himself away. The master asks only one thing of his servants: trade till I come. Life is not intended to be buried or hidden. It is meant to be risked in the deep waters of human love and pain. The master is not concerned about comparing or measuring one person's gifts with those of another. It is not the quantity of results but the quality of risk which is the measure of a faithful servant.

The parable of the wise and foolish virgins has the same message. This story is sometimes interpreted as praise for cautious planning and the search for security. This interpretation is not surprising because prudence is often misunderstood as caution or the search for safety. In the context, however, it is clear that Jesus was talking about prudence as part of the spirit of watchfulness and, therefore, not as caution but as responsible risk. He was trying to tell us that in the key moments of life, we must burn our own oil, not someone else's. Prudence is the earthy wisdom of common sense. It is the willingness to trust our gifts and to take responsibility for them. There are some things that other people can do for us. They can help us and support us, they can trust us and pray for us, they can go to work for us and, at certain times, they can even stand in for us. But in the essential things we ourselves must act. In the crucial events of our lives we must burn our own oil. No one else can hope for us or love for us, no one else can sing our song or free the creative power that is within us. No one else can gamble our gift for us. The authentic meaning of Christian prudence is responsible risk. Real prudence is based on courage, not fear, on the leap of trust rather than the security of caution.

Trust of self is one side of the circle of life. We cannot share our gift until we have received our lives. We cannot give ourselves to other men unless we first accept ourselves from God. The first act of love is an act of hope. The first act of giving is the willingness to receive. The first relationship is the primordial bond which I must forge with my own selfhood.

But trust of self is only one dimension of the circle of life. Self-acceptance is incomplete and perhaps impossible without the experience of trust in and from others. Trust of self is the inward music of hope. Without it, there is only the silence of despair. But the music cannot remain locked inside; it must be sung. Self-acceptance is a melody written for at least two parts. It waits for the sound of another melody. It only becomes the music of life when it is sung in harmony. Trust is not a solo but a symphony—a chorus of voices that blend into one hymn of praise. Self-discovery can only take place in relationship to others. To discover myself is actually to let myself be discovered in the presence of another's trust. Trust of self is an affirmation that life is "ecstatic"—that is, it "breaks out" of itself and expresses itself in relationship to other people. It also unfolds and opens itself to be nourished by the trust and acceptance of others.

The clearest sign that one trusts himself is that he can en-trust his life to others. Similarly, the highest expression of courage is the willingness to en-courage those with whom we share life. If courage is to act from the heart, then to en-courage is to share the trust of our hearts by sharing that power with others.

Tsei Hu affirmed his hope in God by entrusting it to another human being. When he spoke his trust to me, he created a bond that became a source of confidence inside of me, also. Trust creates trust. There is no personal force as strong as the gift of trust. It is literally *evocative*, that is, it "calls out" from the other a response of hope in return. Gustave Thibon describes the power of love in terms that parallel this creative force: "The love of a creature can create nothing in us. But it can *liberate* everything. Without another's intervention, without external warmth, our greatest strength remains forever impotent, forever in chains. Who has ever touched his own depths without the help of another, without being able to say to friend or lover: You gave me to myself, I received my soul at your hands?"[2]

What Thibon says of love can also be said of trust. To trust another is to liberate his power to trust in return. Self-confidence manifests itself in the confidence we have toward one another. Self-acceptance expresses itself in the stance of openness which at once affirms another and receives another.

Our age is not an age of trust. The perimeter of confidence grows daily more narrow. It is not just that we cannot walk the streets at night, or that it is not safe to pick up hitchhikers, or to talk to strangers. Our lives, even in their secure dimensions, have become permeated with feelings of mistrust. The technology of communication has never been so highly developed. Yet, it only serves to point up the mistrust that surrounds our lives. We have hot lines between superpowers in order to prevent accidental global destruction. The airways are filled with sounds but often they are the sounds of silence.

The Russian poet Yevtushenko has described our era as the return of the ice age. He is speaking not in the geological sense but in psychological and spiritual terms. We are growing cold inside because of our inability to make contact with one another. We are dying from the cold of mistrust. Yevtushenko sees the poet as one who establishes contact again between human icebergs:

> I want to be a mail boat for everyone divided by the
> ice of estrangement, a craft before the coming of
> large navigation, moving through the drifting ice
> with letters and parcels.[3]

A Christian is a poet of trust. He attempts to translate the restless dreams of men into personal commitments. He seeks to enflesh the aspirations of his brothers and sisters, as well as his own. He strives to take the hope men have in things and transform it into trust between people.

This is not the kind of task or mission that will make headlines. Tsei Hu accomplished no great political feats. But he did something far more important. He transformed a bed of despair into a place of trust. All of these quiet acts of trust move toward building a community of trust that transcends societal and political structures. We cannot see the ripples of trust as they move out into the lives of others but they are a powerful spiritual presence in the world today.

I believe that the most important time of Tsei Hu's life took place during his last months. During that year-and-a-half when the world of medicine and of man pronounced him incurable, I believe he was doing his share to cure the alienated heart of the world. The most significant events in our lives are not the ones recorded in our family scrapbooks or in newspaper clippings. It is the quality of our trust, not the quantity of our deeds that will give hope to the world. No one of us can hope alone, for hope is not a virtue of the isolated. People can despair alone, but they discover hope only with others.

We bring each other to hope by trusting one another and by encouraging one another. There are days when we must be literally carried to hope and to God. One of the most moving stories of hope in the gospel is the story of the paralytic brought by his friends to Jesus to be healed. It is not so much a story of one man but of a man and his companions who loved him. Together they had decided to bring their friend to the Lord. They allowed no obstacle to stand in their way. I find myself smiling as I picture them climbing the roof and stripping off the tiles. I see the amazed faces of the crowd and of Jesus. Jesus usually worked miracles only in response to the faith of a suffering person. In this instance, Jesus is moved far more by the trust and concern of the man's friends than by the condition of the man himself. The account of St. Luke is quite explicit in this regard: "Seeing *their* faith, Jesus said: 'My friend, your sins are forgiven you'" (Luke 5, 20). Jesus accepted and healed the paralytic in response to the love and trust of his friends.

This is a story of courage because it is an example of encouragement. The bonds of trust become the basis of healing. There are dimensions of our lives that are often paralyzed. There are times when we are immobilized by fear or discouragement. Of our own volition we cannot bring ourselves in trust to the Lord for his healing. We need to be "carried" by the trust and encouragement of those who care for us.

St. Paul brings one of his letters to a close with this simple exhortation: "Give encouragement to each other, and keep strengthening one another . . ." (I Th 5:11). Paul was not just giving pious advice when he wrote these words. From his own experience he knew that he could not find God or continue to grow in hope without the support of others. I came to understand St. Paul more clearly because of my relationship with Tsei Hu. In some respects their lives were alike. Saul of Tarsus also had his life turned around by an "accident" on the highway. When Saul collided with the risen Lord on the road to Damascus he suddenly found his status and his prestige stripped from him. He awoke blind and helpless. Saul, the self-righteous Pharisee, died there in the dust of the road. Paul, the apostle, had to be led by the hand into the city with the help of his friends. He was given his sight and the beginning of a new life only when Ananias reached out to touch him as a brother. Saul became Paul only through the powerful love of God and the encouragement of those who carried him to hope.

Christians are called to be a community of trust and encouragement. We need to know that there are those around us who will lead us to life and carry us to hope. We need to know that there are friends who will be with us on the road; that there will be an Ananias in the city and a community who will stand by us. We need to know the confidence of someone like Tsei Hu. We need to know that the real word for hope is trust.

Chapter Six

AT THE END OF GOD'S PARADE

Hope and Laughter

On one of the side streets of Rome is stationed a gentle old lady named Angelina who sells candy and roasted chestnuts. But she is more than a street vendor. She is, as her name implies, an *angel*, a messenger of the Lord. Angelina messages the life and joy of God to men. She gives the gift of hope and laughter to everyone she meets. Her inner vitality contradicts the external circumstances of her life. She is destitute and lives in a hovel on one of Rome's back alleys. Her health is failing and there are times when her smile cannot hide the pain. Suffering is also part of Angelina's message. It is as expressive of her life as is her joy. Her life is as open and transparent as her smile. She knows that she has nothing to hide—not even the pain. That is the miracle of Angelina. She is happy, not in spite of poverty and pain, but in the midst of them. It isn't that she forces a smile for the sake of doing business. Her smile is not a mask she wears for her customers; it is the look of her heart. Angelina wears her heart on her face. The lines of her face converge at the edges of her mouth where they form a lively pattern of wrinkles which move, like her heart, up toward the sky. Her smile is written in the language of hope.

I often wondered where Angelina found her strength and vitality. One day I asked her what made her so happy and open to life. She answered simply: "God is my laughter." There are many people who would smile condescendingly at this response. They would consider Angelina's statement to be pious but naive. They would praise her for her simplicity but pity her for her ignorance. How can God be the laughter of our lives when there is so much pain? How can he be the hope of our existence when people all around us are suffering? How can there be joy when the innocent are filled with anguish? How can we be open to life when we experience the mystery of evil as it invades our lives?

I am certain that Angelina could not answer these questions. She is not a theologian, but in my estimation she comes very close to being a saint. Angelina has discovered the gigantic secret of joy. Her life is rooted in the belief that we can risk losing everything in the hope of finding the diamond of joy hidden in the soil of human experience. Her outlook on life and her hopeful vision reflect the reason Jesus gave for coming among men: "I have come so that they may have life and have it to the full" (Jn 10:10). Angelina could not deliver a theological lecture on the problem of good and evil, but her life sings its own song about being fully alive. Her message is inscribed on her heart and enfleshed in her life.

God wants to be the laughter of every human heart. Often we are not ready for the gift he wishes to share with us. We have our own understanding of what is necessary to be happy. We have our own definition of the good life to which we cling desperately, even as we experience its emptiness. Our lives are heavy with too many questions about joy, too many doubts about the goodness of God. There are so many objective reasons to be sad, so many excuses for depression. Why talk about having life to the full? Why talk about losing your life for the sake of the good news?

We are uncomfortable with taking Jesus literally. When he tells us that he has come to bring us life, we are tempted to believe that he is speaking of a vague spiritual existence, a life that will come only hereafter, a life that exists only beyond the ambiguity of joy and pain. Only a heart as open and alive as Angelina's is willing to take Jesus at his word. Her response to life is a song of joy. Her presence is a parable of hope. She tells us with her smile that we can trust life. We can trust the purifying as well as the healing forces that engulf us. The search for happiness need not take the form of a desperate search to avoid pain. Angelina is not spending her life in an attempt to separate joy from sorrow or comedy from tragedy. She is not concerned about being happy; she is concerned about *living*. The result is that she is one of the happiest people I have ever met. She is in tune with the music of creation.

She approaches life with a vision of faith and embraces it with hope.

Angelina exemplifies the good news which is at the heart of the gospel. It is the news that life can be embraced as a total experience, that joy is more powerful than sorrow, and that laughter will have the last word. Jesus tells us with his words and by his life that we reach the fullness of meaning only by opening ourselves to *all* of life. The good news is that the strength of our joy does not depend on its being separated from our pain.

The willingness to experience life as permeated with both joy and sorrow contradicts the usual stance of men. Those who take the gospel seriously enough to laugh are a disturbing puzzle to those who have decided that life is a tragedy. For many people, Angelina is more than a pleasant old lady; she is an enigma. Most people strive to avoid pain at all cost. If they cannot avoid it, they are at least careful to separate it from their experiences of joy. They divide their lives into compartments in an attempt to blunt the pain and enhance the pleasure.

Early in his history man began separating comedy from tragedy. The classical theater masks reflect this tendency to separate joy and pain. We often try to divide life into the good days and the bad days. We usually do so on the basis of external circumstances. The criterion for joy or sadness becomes the weather or the time of the year or the influence of external events on our inner feelings. The pursuit of happiness becomes a frantic search to prolong the pleasurable moments and to avoid the painful ones. We try to ride the crest of the good days and grit our teeth through the bad ones. We withdraw into ourselves in an attempt to blunt the jagged edges of life.

For some reason we think that if we separate our joy from our pain we will have more control over them. The truth is quite different. Once joy is separated from pain it often degenerates into a make-believe happiness. If joy is removed from the creative tension of sorrow, it becomes only a surface giddiness. If it is removed from the purifying strength of suffering, it must resort to hollow laughter. It is more light-headed than light-hearted. It becomes childish because it loses its childlike roots in the fabric of real life. The man who refuses to walk through the darkness can only whistle at life as it hurries by. He may be able to force a snicker at life's incongruities, but he will never know the freedom of a great belly laugh which arises from the depth of life.

When joy and sorrow are separated, it is sadness which becomes the dominating force. "The mass of men," wrote Thoreau, "lead lives of quiet desperation." When joy and sorrow are separated, sorrow becomes a pervasive mood and joy only an occasional distraction. Life unfolds like a poorly written play. It is not really lived, it is endured. The brave new world becomes the grave old world. It is no accident that another word for sad is grave, for sadness, apart from joy, is close to death.

Men have discovered the law of gravity.

The human mind can take credit for unveiling the scientific law of gravity. The wisdom of man can also lay claim to discovering the heaviness of the human heart. When joy and pain are separated, there arises what might be called "the human law of gravity." This is the attitude of mind which believes that tragedy is the basic form of the human drama. It says that everything which goes up must come down. Darkness will conquer the light; death will win out in the end. The human law of gravity maintains that whenever we experience joy we must be on our guard, for it is sure to be followed by sorrow. If we have a good day today, we must be prepared for sadness tomorrow. The human law of gravity looks upon joy as "comic relief." It thinks of the spirit of festivity as a "time out" from the sullen game of life. It claims to look at life realistically, but it allows little room for laughter or for the reality of joy.

The person who lives according to the human law of gravity will often speak of growing up in terms of "getting serious" about life. Usually what is meant by this is that we are expected to let our ideals die or at least compromise them beyond recognition. It is so easy to allow our childlike wonder to fade. We stop looking at sunsets and rainbows. We no longer listen to the sound of rain on the roof. We stop making snowballs and flying kites. We begin to read the gospel as though it were a death sentence. We are uncomfortable with Jesus telling us to model our lives after the birds and the flowers. We are irritated with people like Angelina who don't seem to realize how serious life really is.

Getting serious about life too often means becoming sad about life. We become, in Kazantzakis' description, like grocers—we *weigh* everything. When human experience is calculated on the scale of realism, living becomes just another word for endurance.

A further outcome of the separation of joy and pain is a growing distrust of all forms of joy. We begin to question the spirit of cheerfulness whenever it is encountered. We become suspicious of happiness. When joy and pain are separated we often find ourselves opting for the pain. Eventually, one comes to expect sadness, even to depend on it. Melancholy becomes an excuse for a life of complaining and of self-pity. A person can choose depression for so long that feelings of elation come as a psychic shock. For the pessimist life is harsh, but at least it is consistent. Life is sad, but at least it is secure. Happiness is a threat to the man of despair. For the pessimist the only thing worse than a prophet of doom is a prophet of joy. Joy is a threatening experience because it demands hope, and hope demands taking responsibility for choosing a different stance before life.

Human life is more resilient than our attempts to escape from it or to compartmentalize it. Despite our efforts, joy and pain cannot really be driven apart. We are continually invaded by pain and surprised by joy. We are like children who encounter minor accidents on the playground of life. We cry and then go pout in the corner, but our brothers and sisters will not let us alone. In the midst of our tears they call us back to laughter. We have all had the experience of having our tears of self-pity turned into unwilling laughter. It is one more proof that the laughter of God is stronger than the sadness of men.

The fact that tears are an expression of both joy and sorrow is an important clue in our search for the meaning of hope. It tells us that joy and pain are rooted in something deeper in our lives. At times of great intensity our response to joy and pain are often similar. Zorba danced not only when he was happy, but also when he was sad. It enabled him to give expression to his anguish as well as his gladness. The same is true of tears and weeping. Tears are symbols of being alive, of living intensely. We cry when we are in pain *and* when we are filled with joy. Those who do not allow themselves to be uproariously happy or profoundly sad will seldom cry, but it is diffcult to know if they are alive. Tears are not a symbol of life's failure but of its intensification. To live life to the full demands that we weep intensely and laugh often. What Christian faith asks of us is not that we find an answer for pain or an excuse for joy, but that we *live* life, that we embrace both the pain and the joy as promises of growth.

Recent studies in the history of drama indicate that comedy and tragedy have the same origin.[1] They are rooted in a primitive religious cult which recalls the story of a mythic hero and his journey. His life is a series of encounters with danger and darkness. After a long struggle with the powers of evil, he is killed, but he breaks through the bonds of death to a new life and returns home to celebrate the victory with his friends. Comedy and tragedy are not separate representations of human experience, but different dimensions of the one journey of man. It is a mistake to consider tragedy as the more noble expression of the human soul and to look upon comedy as a mere superficiality. Comedy is an integral part of tragedy, because it carries the tragic beyond itself toward a transcendent meaning. Comedy and tragedy are creative poles of human experience. "Life does not cease to become comic because somebody dies," writes George Bernard Shaw, "neither does it cease to be tragic because somebody laughs." We achieve authentic joy only if we are willing to enter into the depths of suffering. Laughter is not to be equated with comic relief; it is not an interlude in the midst of human agony. Comedy is beyond tragedy. We can only discover happiness if we have learned how to weep. We can only laugh if we have experienced the depth of sorrow. We can only know the mystery of resurrection if we have journeyed through the dark waters of death.

The other side of the paradox is equally important: without the spirit of gladness suffering becomes an absurdity. There is an old Italian proverb which says: "Senza umorismo, niente di seriozo"— "without humor, nothing can be serious." Without the gift of laughter life's true nobility is reduced to mere fatality. Without openness to hope there can be no true experience of life. Without the laughter of God we die inside.

Jesus does not separate joy from sorrow. He does not approach the human condition tentatively and then decide whether he will play the role of tragedy or comedy. He is not an actor who chooses to play only selected roles in the human adventure. He is a full participator in the struggle of life. For Jesus, life is not a stage, it is a journey—a journey that includes both the depth of sorrow and the height of joy.

Jesus discovered the law of levity.

In contrast to the human law of gravity, there is the Christian law of levity. The Christian law of levity is a vision which enables man to see beyond the tragic in his life. It is a reminder that man needs the laughter of God to prevent him from taking the world too seriously. The Christian law of levity says that whatever falls into the earth will rise again. Whatever is destroyed in death can, through the power of God, be brought to new life. The Christian law of levity maintains that death is not a dead end, that sorrow will not have the final word.

Jesus is the enfleshment of the Christian law of levity. He shapes its mystery and celebrates its paradox; he communicates it to men through his teaching and his life. In the sermon on the mount Jesus gives us the main outlines of the law of levity. We have traditionally referred to Jesus' words as "the beatitudes," but the term betrays a subtle influence of the human law of gravity. In translating the teaching of Jesus with the term "blessed" we have lessened the power of his message. The word "blessed" literally means *happy*, but a long history of grim lives of the saints has given an entirely different connotation to the word. We don't often think of blessed people as joyful people. We don't easily equate holiness with happiness. For some reason we find it easier to live with sad saints than with joyful followers of Christ. Today we are rediscovering the bond between holiness and wholeness, between being blessed and being happy. The translation found in the Jerusalem Bible recaptures the spirit of the law of levity:

> How happy are the poor in spirit;
> theirs is the kingdom of heaven.
> Happy the gentle:
> they shall have the earth for their heritage.
> Happy those who mourn:
> they shall be comforted.
> Happy those who hunger and thirst for what is
>   right:
> they shall be satisfied.
> Happy the merciful:
> they shall have mercy shown them.
> Happy the pure in heart:
> they shall see God.
> Happy the peacemakers:
> they shall be called sons of God.
> Happy those who are persecuted in the cause
>   of right:
> theirs is the kingdom of heaven.
>
> Mt 5:3–10

Jesus did more than talk about the paradoxical relationship between joy and sorrow; he lived it. The life of Jesus is a reminder that Good Friday cannot be separated from Easter Sunday. If they are looked upon as distinct experiences they lose their meaning. In the past several centuries there has been a tendency for many believers to become Good Friday

Christians, and thereby to miss the power and significance of the resurrection.

The passover journey of Jesus establishes the validity of the Christian law of levity. "I have told you this so that my own joy may be in you and your joy be complete" (Jn 15:11). It is not the seriousness of man which makes hope possible but the levity of God. The levity of God is stronger than the gravity of man; his laughter is more powerful than our sadness; his humor is wiser than our seriousness. It is God's little ones—like Angelina—who understand the Christian law of levity. It enables them to say with true wisdom: "God is my laughter."

God's laughter is not a mocking, bitter sense of ridicule. It is a gentle acceptance of the human condition. It is present wherever men celebrate life with a sense of humor. Humor is the smile hope wears on its face. Humor is the playfulness of hope. If a man has hope, the contradictions of life become incongruities, and the incongruities become events in which one is surprised by God. The laughter of God is the power within us which transforms the tears of sorrow into tears of joy. Laughter is the narrow escape into life. The Christian can afford to look foolish in the eyes of the world. He can even appear ludicrous (i.e., "full of play"). For what else is hope except the gentle laughter of faith in the face of despair? Hope is the way a Christian enfleshes the laughter of God in his life. Hope is the form that the law of levity takes in a Christian's search for fulfillment.

The laughter of God can be heard throughout the

history of salvation. In contrast to the pagan myths which picture the gods creating man as a plaything, the book of Genesis portrays Yahweh creating out of love. When God creates he is not acting capriciously. He does not create man in order to make sport of him. Man is not the victim of divine sarcasm. God creates in order to initiate a relationship of love. The author of Genesis puts it in a more playful way; he hints that God created man so that he could walk with him in the cool of the afternoon. God creates man to become a companion in the playfulness of life. He invites man to become a participator in creativity.

The laughter of God is also manifest in the way he chooses men. How else can we understand God's choosing Jacob over Esau? Or the call of Jonah, the reluctant prophet? How else can we understand Jesus' choice of his disciples? Or the call of Saul of Tarus? How else can we understand God's choosing us? How else can we understand the mysterious ways of God's initiative, except as one side of his divine laughter, or, if you will, his sense of humor? God accepts the human condition better than we do. He loves our incongruities. God's response to man's contradictions are the gifts of acceptance and forgiveness. Faith enables man in turn to accept God's love for him. When man can smile at himself with the laughter of God, he discovers the secret of hope.

God's laughter has the last word over man's despair. Abraham and his wife, Sarah, gave up on God's promise of a child. When Sarah was told that she would soon be pregnant, she laughed in disbelief. But God had the last laugh. A son was born to them in their old age and the human laughter of despair was turned into the divine laughter of love. They named their son Isaac—"Laughter," for he was a sign of the triumph of God's levity over the gravity of man.

Laughter flows from the celebration of incongruity. There could be nothing more incongruous in the Hebrew religious tradition than the incarnation of the Word of God. God spoke to man in many different ways in the history of salvation, but his last word is Jesus. We might put it another way. God's laughter manifested itself in many different ways, but Jesus is God's final laughter. Jesus is God's final and total acceptance of the human condition. God's laughter is not a joke which God plays on man, but the loving act of salvation. If man can accept the person of Jesus his heart will be filled with the laughter of the Father. "You are sad now but I shall see you again and your hearts will be full of joy and that joy, no one shall take from you" (Jn 16:22).

It appears to be a contradiction to speak of Jesus as the laughter of God. Nowhere in the gospel does it say explicitly that Jesus laughed or manifested the emotion of joy. But we miss the central message of the good news if we fail to realize that Jesus' life is an expression of the laughter of God. While men were taking themselves seriously, Jesus trusted in the wisdom of his Father. While the world engaged in the law of gravity, Jesus entrusted himself to the levity of the Father's love. The crowds accused John the Baptist of being possessed because of his asceticism. They called Jesus a drunkard and a glutton because he attended banquets and shared life with the outcasts of society. Jesus knew that the sullenness of men prevented them from being surprised by the newness of God. He must have had an understanding smile on his face when he asked: "What description, then, can I find for the men of this generation? What are they like?" Jesus answered his own question by quoting an ancient proverb: "They are like children shouting to one another while they sit in the market place: 'We played the pipes for you, and you wouldn't dance; we sang dirges, and you wouldn't cry' " (Lk 7:31–32).

Jesus is pointing out that we can't win if we try to understand life only from the narrow vantage point of the human law of gravity. He calls us to view life from a different horizon. He shares the secret of the Father's law of levity: "Wisdom has been proved right by all her children" (Lk 7:35). The Father will have the last laugh.

In the history of Christian art and culture Jesus has appeared in a variety of images. In the catacombs he was the good shepherd; in the great basilicas of the Middle Ages he was the pantocrator and the king of heaven and earth; in the late renaissance he appeared as the crucified savior. Since then he has appeared in many other roles. He has been a rabbi, an enlightened moral teacher, a helpless child in the manger, and a social revolutionary. Recently, the figure of Jesus appeared in the rock musical *Godspell* in the suit of a clown. This may not be the most significant image of Christ in the gospel; it is certainly not the only image. But perhaps it is the most appropriate garment that Jesus could wear in our age. We live in a time that is committed to the human law of gravity. Perhaps no other era in history has taken itself so seriously. No other age has so needed the Christian law of levity. The world longs to hear the laughter of God and to recognize the smile of joy in the mirror of its experience.

The original clown suit is the human condition. When the Word became flesh, he took on the incongruities and contradictions of man. Although the gospels do not picture Christ as laughing or joking, he nevertheless shares many of the characteristics of a clown. A clown is a person who is willing to become a fool for the sake of others. A clown has the quality of resiliency; he is a figure with come-back power. Children are familiar with Bozo the clown. Bozo is a toy clown that has many of the characteristics of real clowns. He is weighted in such a way that he has a natural ballast. He is mobile and is able to be knocked about in all directions. But no matter how hard he is hit he returns to an upright position. The secret is in the stability of his feet. A clown is someone who always comes back up. He has trust as a ballast. He is rooted in the earth. He is anchored in hope. The clowns in the movie cartoons have this same quality of resiliency. In one frame they are blown up by a bomb or flattened by a truck, but in the next frame, they are back on their feet prepared for the next adventure.

It might help us to understand the surprise and joy of the gospel if we viewed it from the perspective of God's laughter. It is certainly incongruous to compare the risen Lord to Bozo, the clown. But perhaps the comparison has some justification when we reflect on the many ways that Jesus manifests himself in our lives. He is the most resilient person who ever lived. He breaks the human law of gravity. He cannot be put off or put down. He is the God of surprises, the Spirit who blows where he wills. Jesus turns our water into wine, our loaves and fishes into a banquet. He surprises us on the road to Emmaus. He breaks through the locked doors of our fears. He appears on the shores of our lives after we have given up and gone fishing. Like John we find ourselves saying in disbelief: "It is the *Lord.*" Is there anything more contradictory to the human law of gravity than the resurrection of Jesus? The risen Lord is the laughter of God erupting from the tomb. The ascension is the final proof of the law of levity. The coming of the Spirit at Pentecost is the sharing of the laughter of God with all men.

To wear the clown suit of redeemed humanity is to remake the contradictions of human life into a new suit of clothes. The human condition becomes an Easter garment.

Clowns are gentle jesters. They "poke fun" rather than hatred. Their laughter is sensitive to man's fragility. They are not putting down the human condition; they are "laughing it up." Their lives hum with a gentle irony rather than with the bitterness of sarcasm. Jesus, in his own way, shared this sense of irony, this suggestion of the gentle mocker. The picture of Jesus which emerges in the gospels is that of a divine troubadour. "Foxes have holes and the birds of the air have nests, but the Son of Man has nowhere to lay his head" (Mt 8:20). This man who frequented parties, who spent time with outcasts, who rode into Jerusalem on a donkey, is a man whose gentleness mocks the false pretensions of power which surrounded him. Romano Guardini believes that the life of Jesus can be summarized in three words: "He passed by." The style of Jesus' life is that of a journey, a passage. It is a journey of hope, and where there is hope there is laughter. Those who wish to walk in the footsteps of God's troubadour must journey with this same hope. Chesterton, writing about the mystery of joy, has sketched a remarkable image of the Christian wayfarer: "The mass of men have been forced to be gay about the little things but sad about the big ones. Nevertheless . . . it is not native to man to be so. Man is more himself, a man is more manlike when joy is the fundamental thing in him and grief the superficial. Melancholy should be an innocent interlude, a tender and fugitive frame of mind. Praise should be the permanent pulsation of the soul. Pessimism is at best an emotional half holiday. Joy is the uproarious labor by which all things live."[2]

A Christian's sense of humor is not an attempt to be frivolous about suffering. Jesus did not approach the human condition as though it were trivial. He did not laugh at the tear-stained face of man. He penetrated beneath the pain to create the radiant countenance of resurrected man. A Christian is formed and shaped in the image of Jesus. He is clothed in the love and power of the risen Lord. He is challenged by Paul to "put on Christ," just as Jesus put on the clown suit of humanity.

Paul knew what it meant to be a wayfarer of Christian hope. The long years of struggle had created in him a spirit of festivity regarding God's wisdom and a sense of humor about his own inadequacies. Paul knew his incongruities; he wrestled with his contradictions. He spoke of glorying in his weakness and of boasting of his failures. He described himself as one born out of the normal course of events. For Paul, the process of becoming a Christian involves the rejection of the human law of gravity with its self-justifying seriousness and its rational explanations. It is the call to become a disciple of God's foolishness: "If anyone thinks of himself as wise, in the ordinary sense of the word, then he must learn to be a fool before he really can be wise. Why? Because the wisdom of this world is foolishness to God" (I Cor 3:18–19). On one occasion Paul described the Christian life in images that might provide a script for a biblical cartoon: "We prove we are God's servants by our purity, knowledge, patience and kindness; by a spirit of holiness, by a love free from affectation; by the word of truth and by the power of God; by being armed with the weapons of righteousness in the right hand and in the left, prepared for honour or disgrace, for blame or praise; taken for impostors while we are genuine; obscure yet famous; said to be dying and here are we alive; rumoured to be executed before we are sentenced; thought most miserable and yet we are always rejoicing; taken for paupers though we make others rich, for people having nothing though we have everything" (II Cor 6:6–10).

Like other clowns Paul has come-back power. He has the resiliency of hope. He knows how to fall, for he is anchored in trust. He has love for a ballast.

There must have been some of the laughter of God in Paul's eyes when he invited his fellow Christians to become fools. There must have been some of the foolishness of Christ in his heart when he wrote: "But it seems to me that God has put us apostles at the end of his parade . . ." (I Cor 4:9).

Chapter Seven

PEOPLE WILL BUY FIELDS
IN THIS LAND AGAIN
Hope and Fidelity

In the year 587 B.C. the city of Jerusalem moved toward the edge of despair. King Zedekiah had run out of military strategies; the government had exhausted its political options. Long years of moral corruption had weakened the spirit of the people. The Babylonians, under King Nebuchadnezzar, had moved in to surround the city. Their siege was slow and deliberate. They waited with the certainty that it would only be a matter of time. Most of the nobility and the affluent were already gone—some had been carried off by the Chaldeans; others, sensing that the end was near, had fled from the city of their own accord. Jerusalem was already fallen in spirit. The soul of the city was in exile long before its citizens were carried off to a foreign country. They had already alienated themselves from God; they had already cut themselves off from hope.

Jeremiah of Anathoth, prophet and man of God, was imprisoned in the king's palace. His prophecies of doom had become an intolerable reminder to the political powers that still remained in Jerusalem. Despite the fact that the king respected Jeremiah, he had taken the precaution of having him confined to the Court of the Guard. For years, Jeremiah had warned his fellow Jews about their infidelity. For years, he had confronted them for worshiping idols and oppressing the poor, for resorting to political manipulation and military intrigue. The fact that his warnings were now coming true only made Jeremiah more despised. He might have been consoled that his prophecies were based on the truth of history. But Jeremiah felt no comfort. He experienced only the pain of seeing his city about to collapse and his people in flight.

Then it happened. Jeremiah was approached by his cousin Hanamel from his home town of Anathoth. Hanamel offered Jeremiah the opportunity to buy a field near their ancestral village, which, at this time, was already in occupied territory. Perhaps Hanamel was in need of money. Perhaps he wanted to join those who were already fleeing from the city and its surroundings. For whatever reason, Hanamel was about to abandon his land, and, as next of kin, Jeremiah had the right under ancient Hebrew law to "redeem" the field—to purchase it for himself. With the vision of a prophet and the sensitivity of a man on fire with God, Jeremiah read Hanamel's invitation as a sign from Yahweh. He heard it as a call to renewed commitment and fidelity. Deliberately observing the public ritual for the transfer of property, Jeremiah put together what little money he had left and purchased the field for seventeen silver shekels.

From the point of view of a casual observer there was nothing unusual about the transfer of the land. The meeting was just another business transaction; the field just another piece of property. But under the circumstances the event took on far-reaching implications. The transaction became a dramatic commitment to fidelity and hope; the field became a symbol of Israel and its future. In the face of despair, Jeremiah performed an act of hope. At a time of moral collapse, he responded with a gesture of faithfulness. On the verge of exile his life spoke of restoration. In the face of military might, Jeremiah bought a field. He staked his life and his future on the words which he heard Yahweh speaking to him: "People will buy fields and vineyards in this land again" (Jer 32:15).

The message of a prophet is inscribed in his flesh before it is revealed in his words. The life of a prophet is itself a message, a revelation of the presence of the Lord. Prophets often employ nonverbal gestures to communicate their message. Jeremiah used many symbolic actions in his life: wearing a loincloth, visiting a potter, putting on a yoke of rope. All of these were means of revealing the call of God in daily experience. Jeremiah used many symbolic actions, but his purchasing of the field had implications that speak directly to our age. Today, when our earth is threatened, when our future is in doubt, when we feel exiled from the earth, Jeremiah's action becomes a powerful symbol of hope and fidelity.

Jeremiah's commitment to hope touches a deep

source of meaning in my life. Perhaps it is because my roots are in the earth, and that I carry within me the strong, deep memories of the days in the fields under the open sky. Perhaps it is because I remember the warmth of the sun and the smell of the earth as full of promise. Perhaps it is because working the land created a bond in me with the earth. Whatever the reason, I cannot think of a more meaningful act of hope for our age than Jeremiah's choice to stake his future on a field. Scarlett O'Hara, the heroine of *Gone with the Wind*, believed that if everything else fell apart, she could always return to Tara, her family estate. The name Tara is close to *terra*—the earth. If everything else fails, we can always go back to the earth. It is the primordial experience of the Lord's presence; it is the promise of every person's future.

How are the historical circumstances of Jeremiah parallel to our own? What can the story of Jeremiah say to us about Christian hope and fidelity? What is the meaning of his symbolic action for 20th century man? More importantly, what is the basis for Jeremiah's fidelity? Where does he derive the vision and the courage to make such an act of hope, such a commitment to faithfulness?

The city of Jerusalem in the 6th Century, B.C., is not unlike the city of man in the 20th century, A.D. The human community is under siege today. We are encircled with the forces of fear; we are hemmed in by the presence of despair. We are in exile on our own planet. Like Jerusalem, the city of man today is dangerously close to the edge of despair. It is not an enemy from another galaxy which has brought us to this point; it is the failure of our own powers of vision. The real energy crisis is not the failure of our natural resources, but the collapse of our moral fiber, the lack of our inward resolve. Our concern about the quality of life is actually a confession of our irresponsibility. The ravaged environment is only an outward expression of our inner wasteland. The crisis today is taking place in the same sphere of experience as it did in the time of Jeremiah—it is a question of hope and fidelity; it is a crisis of human values. Like the citizens of Jerusalem, we often mistake political prowess for human strength; we replace human development with the pursuit of an ever-expanding gross national product; we think that productivity means manufacturing more things, that bigger means better, and that the good life has something to do with the quantity and style of our material possessions. We feel ourselves invaded by the rising tide of pollution. We see our natural resources beginning to disappear. We note with apprehension the spreading blight of famine in the global village. We look for statesmen and we find only politicians; for religious and moral values, and we discover only apathy among people who choose to be comfortable rather than pay the personal price of building a city of justice and peace. Despite our diplomatic words and wishes the arms race continues to spiral upward.

At this point in our history, it is not likely that the citizens of the earth will be carried off to a foreign planet. We cannot stop the earth and get off. This is the only field we have. But many of our fellow citizens have already gone into psychological exile. They have already deserted the city in spirit. There are some who have simply chosen not to look at the problems which press in on us. At a time when the smallest action has public implications, they have chosen to live private lives. Others have been carried off into the land of nostalgia. Because the present is so confusing, because change has taken place with such rapidity, they have withdrawn into a more comfortable and manageable world of memories. In the name of the simple life they have abandoned the task of shaping history.

The experience of psychological exile is even more real on the level of our personal experience than it is in the arena of public issues. Many of us find ourselves wandering aimlessly through a world of personal alienation. We are not at home in our own skins. This is what Phillip Slater meant when he characterized our age as a time when men are engaging in "the pursuit of loneliness"—the flight from responsibility and relationships. The lack of hope in the personal sphere often takes the form of non-involvement. We find it increasingly difficult to make personal commitments. We are reluctant to make promises to anyone, even to ourselves. There has been too much change too soon. The landmarks have disappeared. There are no reference points, no fields in which we can stake the meaning of our lives. When everything around us is in transition, it is difficult to make commitments of any kind, let alone permanent ones. It is even more difficult to remain faithful to the commitments we do make.

The crisis of hope today reveals itself as a crisis

of fidelity. Its impact is felt in those dimensions of our lives that are most sensitive and near to us. The crisis of fidelity affects the intimate world of our personal relationships—our marriages and our families, our friendships and our communities. One of the clearest signs that despair is waiting at the outskirts of our lives is our growing reluctance to make promises and to keep them. In a plastic world promises are reduced to tentative agreements or social arrangements. If life is disposable, so are its commitments. If treaties can be broken, so can personal promises.

But man is a creature who *needs* to make promises. His need to make commitments is as deep as his need to dream. If man dreams of a future without commiting himself to what he sees, his vision is empty and without meaning. Promises are the bread of hope; they nourish our vision of the future, because they challenge us to pay the price of making dreams come true. Without promises our dreams are empty fantasies; they lack the possibility of being rooted in the earth; they are not planted in the field of life.

Fidelity is the way a man keeps his promises. Fidelity is the enduring commitment of hope, the staying power of relationships and the sustaining presence of love. To make a promise is to perform an act of hope, for a promise projects a relationship with another person into a shared future. To commit one's self to share the future is to choose to live in hope. When we can no longer make promises, our lives have fallen into exile. We have become strangers in an alien land.

If the ancient city of Jerusalem is an image of the contemporary city of man, then Jeremiah is a figure of the Christian person of hope. The mood of our age may be that of exile, but the gospel continues to call us to hope. For a Christian, the crisis in the human community is not an excuse for despair but a summons to fidelity. The spirit of Jeremiah is present whenever men choose to remain faithful to the earth and to those with whom they share it.

The Christian community has the mission of calling men to hope and fidelity. The Church is the prophetic presence which confronts the structures of duplicity and despair; it is the community which reconciles those who are alienated from the sources of life and meaning. The task of the Christian is to heal the broken-hearted, to bring good news to the poor, to free the captives, to give sight to the blind, and to proclaim that every age is "the Lord's year of favor" (Lk 4:18).

The prophetic mission begins with the prophet himself. Before he can speak out, he must be purified; before he can heal, he must be reconciled to himself and to God. He cannot call others to fidelity if he is not faithful; he cannot lead others to hope if his spirit is in exile. Before the church can confront the presence of evil in society, it must confront the forces of despair within itself. Before we can heal the broken spirit of the world, we must be at home with the Spirit who dwells in our hearts.

As we reflect on the church's role during these years of change and upheaval, it is clear that we have not always measured up to our prophetic calling. We have reason to be embarrassed by our silence during times of moral urgency. We ought to be uneasy with our lack of courage and compassion. Often we have neither confronted nor consoled. In our fear we have sometimes failed to challenge despair or to be faithful to hope. At times there has been as much cynicism and discouragement within the Christian community as there is anywhere in the city of man. Many Christians have chosen to go into spiritual exile. They have decided, like Hanamel, to sell their land and to leave the city. But in fleeing from the confusion, they have also abandoned the challenge and the possibility of this age. The flight from the church has occurred at a time when its prophetic voice is most needed.

It has been said with some insight that the church has suffered from too many uncritical lovers and from too many unloving critics. Some Christians have refused to ask any questions, while others have rejected every alternative. The faithful prophet is one who walks the narrow ridge between blind loyalty and open-eyed despair. The faithful servant is a loving critic, a loyal questioner. Uncritical lovers are not faithful to the purifying demands of the gospel —they would rather be blindly optimistic than deliberately hopeful. Unloving critics are not faithful to the presence of the Spirit in the midst of human failure—their anger consumes their hope, their zeal destroys their love. An act of confrontation is valid only if it is accompanied by the spirit of acceptance and faithfulness. If a prophet separates himself from his people, he can no longer lead them to hope; he can only join them in despair or withdraw into self-righteous isolation. Beneath his fiery words there must be a steadfast love, an unflinching loyalty. Hope is the power which transforms the anger of confrontation into the spirit of reconciliation. It is for this reason that Jeremiah's decision to purchase the field was so powerful a symbol. His decision validated his years of confrontation because it demonstrated his commitment to the land and to the people he loved.

In one of his poems, Robert Frost describes his stance before life; his image provides an apt description of the role of a Christian prophet:

> And were an epitaph to be my story
> I'd have a short one ready for my own.
> I would have written of me on my stone:
> I had a lover's quarrel with the world.[1]

A Christian is one who has a lover's quarrel with the world. He is engaged in a struggle of hope, a conflict of love. Like Jeremiah, the Christian prophet walks the narrow ridge between capitulation and disillusionment. His love is purified by truth; his criticism is tempered by loyalty. In a lover's quarrel there are no winners or losers—only the honest confrontation of conviction and the search for understanding. A lover's quarrel begins and ends in an atmosphere of fidelity. A prophet's struggle with his people is pursued with intensity, but it is grounded in faithfulness and permeated with love.

There are growing signs of hope in the church today. Quietly, but persistently, the church is carrying forward its prophetic mission. There are many

Christians who are choosing to remain faithful to the task of resistance and reconciliation. They are staking their lives on the enduring covenant of God with his people. They have experienced the loneliness of staying with the church during a painful time of transition, but they are now experiencing a sense of community with others who have made the same radical choice. Together with Jeremiah they believe that "people will buy fields and vineyards in this land again."

There remains a question which we have not yet asked. Jeremiah was a faithful servant, but what was the basis of his fidelity? He was a hopeful prophet, but where did he find the strength to pursue his vision? Where does today's Christian locate the source of his fidelity, the reason for his hope? What sustains our courage during the years of confusion when the people are in flight and the city is in collapse?

The answer to these questions cannot be found within Jeremiah or within any of us; the answer lies in the fidelity of God. Jeremiah was able to make an act of hope because he relied on the faithfulness of Yahweh. Jeremiah was faithful to his people because he knew that God is faithful to his promises. He could stake his future on a field because he trusted that Yahweh would remain faithful to his covenant.

Man can make promises only because God has established an everlasting bond of love with his people. Man can be faithful to the future because God is faithful to all of history. The God of Abraham, Isaac and Jacob is not a far-off God; he is a seeking God who draws near to man and enters into a personal relationship with him. He is the God who initiates a covenant with man and promises to remain faithful: "If Yahweh set his heart on you and chose you, it was not because you out-numbered other peoples: you were the least of all peoples. It was for love of you and to keep the oath he swore to your fathers that Yahweh brought you out with his mighty hand and redeemed you from the house of slavery, from the power of Pharaoh king of Egypt. Know then that Yahweh your God is God indeed, the faithful God who is true to his covenant and his graciousness for a thousand generations towards those who love him and keep his commandments . . . " (Dt 7:7–9).

The faithfulness of man is a reflection of the fidelity of God. Our commitment to life is rooted in the promise of God. Fidelity is the form hope takes as it walks into the future.

A Christian cannot speak of fidelity without speaking of Jesus. The vision which sustained Jeremiah is fulfilled in Christ's fidelity to his Father. The fulfillment of the divine promise transcends the vision of the prophets of Israel, for it is more than a promise—it is a person. Jesus is the fidelity of God become flesh. Jesus is the faithfulness of the Father to men; he is the expression of the Father's commitment to remain true to his people. "God loved the world so much that he gave his only Son, so that everyone who believes in him may not be lost but may have eternal life" (Jn 3:16).

Jesus, like Jeremiah, is a *redeemer*—he purchases the fallen field of creation, he buys back the exiled city of man. He does so, not with silver shekels, but with his own blood. For the Hebrew, blood is a symbol of life. When Jesus gathered his friends together for the last time, he knew that the price of his fidelity would be nothing less than the total gift of his life. At the last supper he shared with them the cost of his discipleship: "This cup is the new covenant in my blood which will be poured out for you" (Lk 22:20). Blood is another word for that which is deepest in us; it is the price we must pay to redeem the earth and to claim it for hope. For the Christian, there is only one road to fidelity—it is the same path which Jesus walked. It is the passover journey through death to new life. The cost of discipleship is the same for us as it was for Jesus: "If the world hates you, remember that it hated me before you. If you belonged to the world, the world would love you as its own; but because you do not belong to the world, because my choice withdrew you from the world, therefore the world hates you. Remember the words I said to you: A servant is not greater than his master. If they persecuted me, they will persecute you too . . ." (Jn 15:18–20).

We can purchase the field of eternal life, only if we are willing to commit all our energies to the task of resistance and reconciliation. Hope is not an optimistic frame of mind; it is a radical decision of heart. Fidelity is the form hope takes in order to purchase the fallen field of our lives. Such faithfulness requires more than a passing interest or an outward adherence; it demands the free gift of our inner selves. It demands our life's blood.

Jesus is the encounter between the faithfulness of the Father and the hunger of man for hope. In Jesus we have found a faithful brother whose obedience has initiated a new creation and a new humanity. We can be faithful to the future because Jesus has purchased with his own life the new heavens and the new earth. We can hope in the future because the victory has already been won: "The world is standing on tiptoe waiting for the full revelation of the sons and daughters of God" (Rm 8:9, J. B. Phillips translation).

As the Father is faithful in giving us his Son, so Jesus is faithful in sharing the gift of his Spirit. The Spirit is the bond of love between the Father and the Son. Through the gift of the Spirit, Jesus continues to be faithful to the earth and to the church: "Know that I am with you always; yes, to the end of time" (Mt 28:20). The Spirit moves through our lives with his peace and his restless love. He reveals the many ways that God is faithful to his people. The fidelity of God is manifest whenever we are willing to make promises to our brothers and sisters. The fidelity of God is present whenever we commit ourselves to the earth and to the renewal of the human community. The fidelity of God is revealed each time we enter into a covenant of love with another person.

The ancient Hebrews interpreted the rainbow as a sign of God's promises (cf. Gn 9). They looked to the rainbow as a symbol of God's fidelity to his creation, and, in the brightness of this natural wonder, they celebrated God's enduring love for his people. Rainbows are the color of hope. They are symbols of life's promise and possibility; they are invitations to joy; they are creation's way of praising God for his faithfulness. "Man is born with rainbows in his heart," writes Carl Sandburg, "and you'll never read him unless you consider rainbows."[2] If we want to understand the meaning of our lives, if we want to walk into the future with hope—then we must consider the rainbows in our hearts. We are born with an immense longing within us. We are born with promises in our hearts. We are born with the hunger to make commitments and to establish covenants. We are born to be faithful and to celebrate hope. We are born to discover God in the field of creation.

NOTES

Chapter 2

1. For the images and insights of this section I am indebted to Robert L. Short, *A Time to Be Born—A Time to Die* (New York, Harper and Row, 1973), cf. esp. pp. 75–112.

2. Albert Camus, *Neither Victims Nor Executioners* (Chicago, World Without War Publications, 1972), 19.

Chapter 3

1. *"Pastoral Constitution on the Role of the Church in the Modern World,"* Documents of Vatican II, ed. by Walter M. Abbott, S.J. (New York Guild Press, 1966), 199–200.

2. Teilhard de Chardin, *The Phenomenon of Man*, trans. by Bernard Wall (New York, Harper and Row, 1961), 229–231.

3. Archibald MacLeish, "The Revolt of Diminished Man," *The Saturday Review* (Vol. 52, June 7, 1969), 19.

Chapter 5

1. John Berryman, "Eleven Addresses to the Lord," in *Love and Fame* (New York: Farrar, Straus and Giroux, 1970), p. 85.

2. Gustav Thibon, *What God Has Joined Together* (Chicago: Henry Regnery Company, 1952), p. 169.

3. Yevgeny Yevtushenko, *Stolen Apples* (Garden City, N.Y.: Doubleday and Company, 1971), p. XVII.

Chapter 6

1. Many of the images and themes of this section are derived from Joseph C. McLelland, *The Clown & The Crocodile* (Richmond, Va.: John Knox Press, 1970), cf. esp., "Beyond Tragedy—The Comic Vision," pp. 79–86.

2. G. K. Chesterton, *Orthodoxy* (New York: Doubleday & Co., Inc., 1959), p. 159.

Chapter 7

1. Robert Frost, "The Lesson for Today," as found in *The Poetry of Robert Frost* (New York: Holt Rinehart & Winston, 1969).

2. Carl Sandburg, *The People, Yes* (New York: Harcourt, Brace and Company, 1936), p. 208.